Fehlerkiller

Compact Schülerhilfen
Englisch
Unregelmäßige Verben

Alkyone Karamanolis

D1662640

Compact Verlag

© 1993 Compact Verlag
Redaktion: Petra Bachmann
Umschlaggestaltung: Sabine Jantzen
Printed in Germany
ISBN 3-8174-3681-5
34 36811

Inhalt

Wie du mit diesem Buch lernen kannst!

Die unregelmäßigen Verben im Englischen sind nicht schwer zu beherrschen. Man muß sie nur grundsätzlich einüben. Dabei hilft dir dieses Buch.
Du findest die wichtigsten unregelmäßigen Verben alphabetisch geordnet. Nach den verschiedenen Formen – Grundform, Imperfekt, Partizip – werden dir wichtige Redewendungen zu dem betreffenden Verb genannt. Danach stellt dir der lustige Bär eine Aufgabe. Bevor du diese löst, solltest du dir die Formen und Redewendungen gut einprägen.
Die Test machen es dir möglich, das Gelernte zu überprüfen. Übe die Verben, bei denen du noch Schwierigkeiten hast, noch einmal. Wenn du das ganze Buch durchgearbeitet hast, kannst du dich an den Abschlußtest machen.
Alle Lösungen findest du am Schluß des Buches. Bei Lösungen, die mit einem Sternchen versehen sind, gibt es außer der genannten Lösung noch andere mögliche Lösungen.

Nun viel Erfolg beim Lernen!

AE = Amerikanisches Englisch.

| awake | awoke/awaked | awoken/awaked | aufwachen, wecken |

Folgende Redewendung solltest du lernen:
to awake to something
   - sich einer Sache bewußt werden

Füge die korrekte Verbform ein.

1. Songs often ... memories of the past.
2. By talking this way, he surely ... their anger.
3. Yesterday I ... at 2 p.m.

Übersetze:
1. Plötzlich weckte mich ein seltsames Geräusch.
2. Sonntags wachten die Kinder nie vor neun Uhr auf.
3. Als er aufwachte, hatte es aufgehört zu regnen.

Achtung: Es gibt auch das regelmäßig gebildete Verb 'to awaken': z.B. The customer's behaviour awakened her anger.
Wie „awake" wird gebildet:
wake woke/waked woken/waked - aufwachen;wecken

| be | was/were | been | sein |

Folgende Redewendungen solltest du lernen:
to be about to do something
   - im Begriff sein, etwas zu tun
be that as it may
   - sei es wie es wolle, trotzdem

Füge die korrekte Verbform ein.
1. The weather ... lovely yesterday.
2. He ... always ... a good athlete.
3. When we arrived, the guests ... already leaving.
4. You ... right when you said we should better leave.

Übersetze:
1. Er ist zehn Tage in London gewesen.
2. Die Prüfung war für die Schüler ziemlich schwierig.
3. Sie waren bereits in vier Museen.

bear	bore		borne (born)	tragen, ertragen, gebären

Folgende Redewendungen solltest du lernen:
to bear something in mind
    -etwas nicht vergessen; an etwas denken
to bear resemblance to
    - Ähnlichkeit haben mit
to bear up
    - durchhalten; standhalten

Füge die korrekte Verbform ein.
1. He wouldn't ... being treated this way.
2. She ... an only child.
3. The boy was ... in March.
4. We ... all the costs involved until now.

Übersetze:
1. Ich kann diesen Lärm nicht ertragen.
2. Sie ist in Amsterdam geboren.
3. Er trug den Namen seines Vaters.
4. Wann wurdest du geboren?

beat	beat		beaten	schlagen

Folgende Redewendungen solltest du lernen:
That beats everything!
    - Das ist doch die Höhe!
Can you beat it!
    - Das darf doch nicht wahr sein!
to beat about the bush
    - um den heißen Brei herumreden
to beat something into someone
    - jemandem etwas einbleuen
to beat the deadline
    - die Frist einhalten

Füge die korrekte Verbform ein.
1. Children shouldn't be ... .
2. They had to ... a way through the bushes.
3. ... the drum is not as easy as it seems.
4. Their army ... on top of that hill.

Übersetze:
1. Sie schlug mich immer beim Schachspielen.
2. Er schlug mehrmals an die Tür.
3. Er schlug die Trommel.

become	became	become	werden

Folgende Redewendung solltest du lernen:
to become the rule
  - zur Regel werden

Füge die korrekte Verbform ein.
1. The following winter, things ... more difficult.
2. I never knew that he ... a dancer.
3. What could possibly ... of him?
4. When he learned that I wouldn't come to the meeting, he ... furious.

Übersetze:
1. Es wurde wärmer.
2. Schließlich gewöhnte (become accustomed) er sich an das Wetter in Indien.
3. Jeans sind ziemlich teuer geworden.

Achtung: „become" bedeutet nicht dt. „bekommen"

begin	began	begun	anfangen

Folgende Redewendungen solltest du lernen:
to begin with, ...
  - erstens; zunächst einmal ...
well begun is half done
  - gut begonnen ist halb gewonnen
to begin on something
  - etwas in Angriff nehmen

Füge die korrekte Verbform ein.
1. The play ... at 9 p.m.
2. I think he ... already ... studying Spanish.
3. She ... as a chorus girl but now she's famous.
4. At this point I seriously ... worrying about him.
5. They ... saving money for a trip abroad.

Übersetze:
1. Als wir den Fernseher einschalteten, hatte der Film bereits begonnen.
2. Sie fing an, unruhig zu werden.
3. Die Proben fangen im März an.

bend	bent	bent	biegen, beugen

Füge die korrekte Verbform ein.
1. The branch ... heavily when the fat cat jumped upon it.
2. She ... forward and stared at me with a stunned expression in her face.

Übersetze:
1. Er bückte sich, um eine Münze aufzuheben.
2. Sie hatte sich vorgebeugt und hörte uns aufmerksam zu.

bind	bound	bound	binden

Folgende Redewendungen solltest du lernen:
to be bound to do something
  -zwangsläufig etwas tun müssen
that was bound to happen
  - das mußte ja passieren

Füge die korrekte Verbform ein.
1. This book is ... in leather.
2. She ... herself to take care of the old man.

Übersetze:
1. Wir waren zu Diskretion verpflichtet.
2. Der Einbrecher hatte den Hauswirt an den Stuhl gefesselt.

bite	bit	bitten	beißen

Folgende Redewendung solltest du lernen:
to bite back a remark
  - sich eine Bemerkung verkneifen

Füge die korrekte Verbform ein.
1. You could ... been ... badly by that ferocious dog!
2. She ... her lips.

Übersetze:
1. Der Angler wurde böse, weil die Fische nicht anbissen.
2. Der Postbote wurde von einem feindseligen Hund gebissen.
3. Ich habe mir auf die Zunge gebissen.

bleed	bled	bled	bluten

Füge die korrekte Verbform ein.
1. His nose is ...
2. He cut his finger mending the gate; it is ... badly.

Übersetze:
1. Die Wunde blutete so sehr, daß er bewußtlos wurde.
2. Wenn wir nicht sofort einen Arzt rufen, wird er verbluten (to bleed to death).

blow	blew	blown	blasen

Folgende Redewendung solltest du lernen:
to blow one's top
   - vor Wut explodieren, in die Luft gehen

Füge die korrekte Verbform ein.
1. The window ... open and the rain came in.
2. He once ... glass.
3. She got a bleeding nose from ... it all the time.

Übersetze:
1. Der Wind blies die Kerze aus.
2. Der Wind hat ihm den Hut vom Kopf geblasen.

break	broke	broken	brechen

Folgende Redewendung solltest du lernen:
to break up a relationship
   - eine Beziehung beenden

Füge die korrekte Verbform ein.
1. The glass fell down and ... .
2. How did you manage to get this ... ?

Übersetze:
1. Sie hat eine wertvolle Vase zerbrochen.
2. Seine lustige Bemerkung hat das Eis gebrochen.

bring	brought	brought	bringen

Folgende Redewendungen solltest du lernen:
to bring someone down to earth
   - jemandem auf den Boden der Tatsachen zurückholen
to bring about a change
   - eine Veränderung bewirken; mit sich bringen
to bring up children
   - Kinder großziehen

Füge die korrekte Verbform ein.
1. He ... along some wine.
2. We ... this car with us from Portugal.
3. This ring ... me good luck.
4. The orphan ... up by its grandparents.

Übersetze:
1. Ihr Gespräch brachte ihn auf den Boden der Tatsachen zurück.
2. Ich kann nicht wegfahren, weil sie das Auto noch nicht zurückgebracht hat.
3. Komm', und bring" deine Freunde mit!

build	built	built	bauen

Folgende Redewendungen solltest du lernen:
to build one's hopes on
   - seine Hoffnungen setzen auf

Füge die korrekte Verbform ein.
1. I ... my hopes on this project and got terribly disappointed.

2. The church on the hill was ... of wood.
3. Don't ... your hopes on your relations.
4. They ... a house but they never moved in.

Übersetze:
1. Dieses Haus wurde in nur zwei Monaten gebaut.
2. Weißt du, wie die Pyramiden gebaut wurden?
3. Ihre Beziehung war auf Sand gebaut; sie mußte scheitern.
4. Die neue Schule soll nächstes Jahr gebaut werden.

Test 1: Setze alle korrekten Verbformen ein (awake, be, bear, become, begin, bend, bind, bite, bleed, blow, break, bring, build):
1. The students ... studying for their upcoming exam.
2. The pages of this book ... yellowish in the course of time.
3. He ... a slight resemblance to his grandmother.
4. Luckily we managed to ... the deadline.
5. Unluckily he wasn't ... to the danger he was running.
6. She came back from the seaside, badly ... by the mosquitos.
7. Do you know who ... St. Paul's Cathedral?
8. As soon as the actor entered the stage, the audience ... to laugh.
9. The agent ... her to secrecy.
10. He ... his arm on the tenniscourt.
11. After the accident she wasn''t able to ... her knee any more.
12. I never saw a wound ... like this.
13. The only thing he remembers is that a doctor came and ... him.
14. Take care that the wind doesn't ... the papers off the table.
15. I couldn't ... myself to let her down.

Übersetze:
1. Sie stand auf, sobald sie aufwachte (awake).
2. Wir waren wirklich schockiert, als wir von dem Unfall hörten (be).
3. Gestern bekam ich einen Brief, der keine Unterschrift trug (bear).
4. Der Regen schlug die ganze Nacht lang gegen die Fensterscheiben (beat).
5. Er ist Fremdenführer geworden (become).
6. Nur wenige englische Wörter fangen mit 'K' an (begin).
7. Er knickte immer die Seiten seiner Bücher (bend).
8. Der Arzt verband die Wunde (bind).
9. Bist du jemals von einer Katze gebissen worden (bite)?

10. Er blies den Staub vom Buch, schlug es auf der ersten Seite auf und begann zu lesen (blow).
11. Sie brach sich das Bein, als sie in der Badewanne ausrutschte (break).
12. Er brachte immer seine Freundin mit, wenn ich ihm zum Abendessen einlud (bring).
13. Das Meer hat die Sandburg, die wir gestern gebaut haben, weggeschwemmt (build).

burst	burst	burst	bersten, platzen

Folgende Redewendung solltest du lernen:
to burst into laughter/tears
- in Gelächter/Tränen ausbrechen

Füge die korrekte Verbform ein.
1. The car exploded and ... into flames.
2. She ... with laughter when she saw him in this disguise.

Übersetze:
1. Als sie von dem Unfall erfuhr, brach sie in Tränen aus.
2. Er platzte in das Zimmer, ohne anzukopfen.

buy	bought	bought	kaufen

Füge die korrekte Verbform ein.
1. I ... this cupboard during my stay in France.
2. I ... some fish for today's dinner.

Übersetze:
1. Sie werden ein Haus am Meer kaufen.
2. Ich habe die Tickets noch nicht gekauft.

cast	cast	cast	werfen

Folgende Redewendung solltest du lernen:
to be cast down
- niedergeschlagen sein

Füge die korrekte Verbform ein.
1. He always tried ... the blame on me.
2. She ... aside her inhibitions and went to see her aunt.

Übersetze:
1. Sie schoben mir die Schuld für das Scheitern des Plans zu.
2. Ihr Aufsatz warf ein neues Licht auf das Problem des Walfangs.

catch	caught	caught	fangen

Folgende Redewendung solltest du lernen:
to catch one's breath
  - wieder zu Atem kommen; den Atem anhalten

Füge die korrekte Verbform ein.
1. A prisoner had escaped. They ... him in a tavern.
2. At last I ... up with her.

Übersetze:
1. Er fing den Ball und warf ihn mir zurück.
2. Sie haben den Dieb noch nicht gefangen.

choose	chose	chosen	wählen

Folgende Redewendungen solltest du lernen:
We cannot choose but do it
  - Es bleibt uns keine andere Wahl, als es zu tun
not choose to do something
  - nicht geruhen, etwas zu tun

Füge die korrekte Verbform ein.
1. They couldn't ... but go through with the examination.
2. I ... not to accept their invitation.

Übersetze:
1. Der Anzug, den du ausgesucht hast, ist sehr kleidsam.
2. Hast du schon ausgesucht?

cling	clung	clung	sich klammern an

Füge die korrekte Verbform ein.
1. He ... to a faint hope of being rescued.
2. She ... to me and never let me go.

Übersetze:
1. Die Kleider klebten ihm am Leib, weil er durch den Regen gegangen war.

come	came	come	kommen

Folgende Redewendungen solltest du lernen:
to come round
   - bei jemandem kurz vorbeischauen; jemanden besuchen
to come to grips with something
   - sich ernsthaft auseinadersetzen mit etwas
to come to the conclusion that
   - zu dem Schluß kommen; daß
to come to one's senses
   - zur Besinnung kommen; wieder zur Vernunft kommen
to come to the point
   - zur Sache kommen
to come to a head
   - sich zuspitzen (Lage; Situation)
to come to terms with someone
   - sich einigen mit jemandem
to come about
   - geschehen; passieren; zustandekommen
in the years to come
   - in den kommenden Jahren
to come in handy
   - nützlich sein; wie gerufen kommen
to come to terms with something
   - etwas bewältigen, mit etwas fertig werden
come to think of it ...
   - wenn ich es mir so recht überlege
come what may
   - was auch immer geschieht; komme, was wolle
Come off it!
   - Hör schon auf damit! Gib nicht so an! Tu nicht so!

Füge die korrekte Verbform ein.

1. They ... to see us on Tuesday.
2. I am beginning to be worried because she still ... .
3. I don't know what he is talking about. He obviously ...n't yet ... to the point.
4. In the end I ... to terms with my boss.

Übersetze:
1. Er ist gestern abend nicht zu unserer Party gekommen.
2. Als sich der Konflikt zuspitzte, begannen sie endlich zu verhandeln (to enter into negotiations).
3. Er ist gekommen, um seine Koffer abzuholen.
4. Als ich im Krankenhaus war, kam sie mich jeden Tag besuchen.
5. Ich stieß auf dieses Foto (to come across), als ich deine Briefe durchsah.

cost	cost	cost	kosten

Folgende Redewendungen solltest du lernen:
to cost someone dearly
   - jemanden teuer zu stehen kommen
to cost the earth
   - ein Heidengeld kosten
to cost an arm and a leg
   - einen zu hohen Preis haben

Füge die korrekte Verbform ein.

1. The paperback edition doesn't ... half as much as the hardcover edition.
2. This picture ... a fortune some years ago!
3. Writing this book ... me much time.

Übersetze:
1. Das Wettrennen kostete ihn sein Leben.
2. Letztes Jahr haben die Kohlen weniger gekostet.

Beachte: In der Bedeutung „Kosten kalkulieren, veranschlagen', wird die Form „costed" verwendet: 'The working hours were costed at 200 pounds.

creep	crept	crept	kriechen, schleichen

Folgende Redewendungen solltest du lernen:
to make someone's flesh creep
  - jemandem Gänsehaut machen,
   (vgl. to give someone the creeps)
to creep into someone's favour
  - sich bei jemandem einschmeicheln
to creep back
  - wieder angekrochen kommen

Füge die korrekte Verbform ein.
1. The burglar ... silently towards the house.
2. Watching this movie will make your flesh ... .
3. He kept ... back to me.

Übersetze:
1. Leise schlich er sich in das Zimmer.
2. Dein Geigenspiel macht mir Gänsehaut.

cut	cut	cut	schneiden

Folgende Redewendungen solltest du lernen:
to cut down a tree
  - einen Baum fällen
to cut a long story short
  - um es kurz zu machen; kurz und gut
to cut someone dead
  - jemanden „schneiden", links liegen lassen, nicht beachten, völlig ignorieren
to cut someone to the heart
  - jemanden sehr betrüben, ins Herz schneiden
to cut no ice with someone
  - bei jemandem keinen Eindruck machen
to cut someone down to size
  - jemanden zurechtweisen; den Kopf zurechtsetzen
to be cut out for something
  - für etwas wie geschaffen sein
to cut the ground from under someone's feet
  - jemandem den Boden unter den Füßen wegziehen

to cut something down
  - etwas verringern, herabsetzen, einschränken (z.B. Pro-
    duktion, Ausgaben)
Cut it out!
  - Hör auf damit! Laß den Quatsch!

Füge die korrekte Verbform ein.
1. His behaviour ... me to the heart.
2. They ... down the lime-tree when they started building the
    house.
3. She ... into the conversation in a very rude manner.
4. He ... out all the pictures out of the catalogue.
5. I don't think they ... ever ... the grass in their gar-
    den since they moved in.

Übersetze:
1. Ich hatte es so eilig, daß ich mich beim Rasieren ge-
    schnitten habe.
2. Ich schneide alle Zeitungsartikel, die mich interessie-
    ren, aus.
3. Karton ist nicht leicht zu schneiden.
5. Ich habe mir gestern die Haare schneiden lassen.
6. Seit wir den Rasen gemäht haben, können wir wieder im
    Garten sitzen.

Beachte: to cut up (AE) - angeben, Quatsch machen

Test 2: *Setze alle korrekten Verbformen ein (burst, buy, cast, catch, choose, cling, come, cost, creep, cut):*
1. He ... round to see whether we were getting along with it.
2. They ... the burden of the whole affair on me.
3. I ...n't yet ... between the two flats.
4. I'm afraid I ... a cold! When he saw her new car, he ... with envy.
5. You shouldn't ... into the conversation.
6. The suit I bought for my sister's wedding ... me 100 pounds.
7. After his illness he had a hard time ... up with the rest of his class
    at school.
8. Look, we ... the mouse in a trap!
9. Until that day I ... to the belief that he was an honest person despi-
    te everything.
10. He ... into her favour by offering generous presents to her.
11. To catch fish, you have ... nets.

Übersetze:
1. Wenn der Reifen nicht geplatzt wäre, wäre der Unfall nicht geschehen (burst).
2. Er hat sich noch kein Auto gekauft (buy).
3. Als wir sie beschuldigten, das Geld gestohlen zu haben, richtete sie ihren Blick auf den Boden und ging aus dem Zimmer (to cast one's eyes down).
4. Sie erwischten ihn dabei als er versuchte, das Haus in Brand zu stecken (catch).
5. Er hielt den Atem an und schlich sich in das Zimmer (catch).
6. Das Restaurant, das er ausgesucht hatte, war sowohl billig als auch schlecht (choose).
7. Ich mag diesen Hut nicht. Meine Mutter hat ihn für mich ausgesucht (choose).
8. Es blieb ihnen keine andere Wahl als seine Entscheidung zu akzeptieren (choose).
9. Ich klammerte mich an ihren Arm weil ich nichts sehen konnte (cling).
10. Sie kam zurück, um sich zu entschuldigen (come).
11. Letztes Jahr kosteten die Kohlen weniger (cost).
12. Er kroch unter den Tisch, um eine Münze zu suchen, die er verloren hatte (creep).
13. Er schnitt ein riesiges Stück Kuchen ab.

deal	dealt	dealt	(be)handeln

Füge die korrekte Verbform ein.
1. She cheated when she ... the cards.
2. Last year they ... in cars.

Übersetze:
1. Letztes mal hast du die Karten ausgeteilt, diesmal bin ich dran.

dig	dug	dug	graben

Füge die korrekte Verbform ein.
1. They ... up some very embarassing points about his past.
2. They ...n't yet ... up the truth about this crime.

Übersetze:
1. Ihr habt noch nicht tief genug gegraben.
2. Sie haben jahrelang nach Gold gegraben, aber nie welches gefunden.

dive	dived/dove	dived	(ein)tauchen

Beachte: Nur im AE ist die Form „dove" üblich, sonst ist das Verb regelmäßig!

Folgende Redewendung solltest du lernen:
to dive into the crowd
  - in der Menge untertauchen

Füge die korrekte Verbform ein.
1. He ... in a very dangerous place near a sunken ship.
2. They ... for pearls.

Übersetze:
1. Er tauchte ins Meer und blieb vier Minuten unter Wasser.

do	did	done	tun, machen

Folgende Redewendungen solltest du lernen:
to do away with something
  - etwas beseitigen; abschaffen
to do away with someone
  - jemanden töten
to do someone a favour
  - jemandem einen Gefallen tun
to do someone harm
  - jemandem schaden, etwas antun
to be done for
  - erledigt sein; am Ende sein
to do well
  - Erfolg haben; gut abschneiden (z.B. Prüfung)
to do the dishes
  - Geschirr spülen
to do up the house
  - das Haus renovieren, reparieren
to do up one's face
  - sich schminken

Nothing doing!
   - Da ist nichts zu machen; kommt nicht in Frage!
That will do!
   - Das genügt; das reicht!

Füge die korrekte Verbform ein.
1. The gang ... away with the witness.
2. They ...n't ... up their house since they moved in 1932.
3. The dancer ... up his face before appearing on the stage.
4. I didn't mean to ... you harm.
5. You ... your best, didn't you?
6. What ... you been ... during these weeks?
7. He ... the right thing when he left for Australia.
8. Look what you ... to me.
9. She ... well at her last exam.

Übersetze:
1. Er tat sein Bestes, um sie zu retten.
2. Er hat es absichtlich getan.
3. Ich habe das Geschirr noch nicht abgespült.
4. Hast du deine Hausaufgaben gemacht?
5. Was hast du im August gemacht?
6. Du hättest das nicht tun sollen!

Beachte: Das Verb „do" wird auch als Hilfsverb gebraucht!

draw	drew	drawn	ziehen, zeichnen

Folgende Redewendungen solltest du lernen:
to draw apart
   - sich auseinanderleben
to draw someone's attention to something
   - jemandes Aufmerksamkeit auf etwas lenken
to draw something to a close
   - etwas zu Ende bringen, abschließen
to draw near
   - näherkommen (zeitlich und örtlich)

Füge die korrekte Verbform ein.
1. In the course of time, they ... apart.
2. She ... him aside and told him all about it.
3. He ... just ... a very nice portrait of my father.

Übersetze:
1. Ich kann aus ihrer Aussage keinen Schluß ziehen.
2. Sie holte Atem und tauchte ins Wasser.

drink	drank	drunk	trinken

Folgende Redewendungen solltest du lernen:
to drink something away
   - etwas versaufen (Geld)
to drink someone under the table
   - jemanden unter den Tisch trinken
to drink in someone's words
   - jemandes Worte gierig aufsaugen
to drink in the view
   - den Ausblick genießen

Füge die korrekte Verbform ein.
1. He ... all the gin, so there's nothing left for us.
2. I ...n't ... half as much as you, therefore I see things clearer.

Übersetze:
1. Er hätte mich unter den Tisch trinken können, wenn er gewollt hätte.
2. Er ertränkte seine Sorgen im Alkohol.
3. Sie ist gestorben, weil sie zu viel getrunken hat.

drive	drove	driven	fahren, treiben

Folgende Redewendungen solltest du lernen:
to drive someone nuts
   - jemanden wahnsinnig machen
to drive something home to someone
   - jemandem etwas klarmachen
to be driving at something
   - auf etwas hinauswollen; auf etwas anspielen

Füge die korrekte Verbform ein.
1. He ... been ... all night long.
2. His silly behaviour nearly ... me nuts.
3. The storm ... the clouds away; now the sun is shining again.

Übersetze:
1. Er fuhr sehr vorsichtig.
2. Ich habe dieses Auto acht Jahre lang gefahren.
3. Sie riefen die Polizei und fuhren dann weiter.

eat	ate	eaten	essen

Folgende Redewendungen solltest du lernen:
to eat like a horse
   - wie ein Scheunendrescher essen
to eat in/out
   - zu Hause essen/essen gehen
What's eating him?
   - Was für eine Laus ist ihm über die Leber gelaufen? Was hat er denn?

Füge die korrekte Verbform ein.
1. They ... anything since yesterday.
2. We ... out last night.
3. ... you ever ... at an African restaurant?
4. He ... up his soup and left immediately.

Übersetze:
1. Er lud sie nie ins Restaurant ein, weil sie wie ein Scheunendrescher aß.
2. Sie benimmt sich eigenartig; weißt du, was sie hat?
3. Wir begannen zu Hause zu essen, als unser Geld ausging.

fall	fell	fallen	fallen

Folgende Redewendungen solltest du lernen:
to fall in love with someone
   - sich in jemanden verlieben
to fall through
   - nichts werden; ins Wasser fallen

to fall flat
- schiefgehen; danebengehen

Füge die korrekte Verbform ein.
1. He ... from the top of this building; luckily he didn't get injured.
2. Yesterday I ... asleep in class.
3. I knew I would ... in love with him if I kept seeing him.

Übersetze:
1. In der Wüste fällt die Temperatur nachts stark ab.
2. Als der Boxer seinen Gegner sah, sank ihm der Mut.
3. Die Teekanne fiel vom Tisch und brach in Stücke.
4. Ich bin hingefallen und habe mir das Bein gebrochen.

feed	fed	fed	füttern

Folgende Redewendungen solltest du lernen:
to feed at the breast
- Kind stillen
to feed on something
- etwas essen, sich ernähren von
to feed someone up
- jemanden aufpäppeln
to be fed up with something/someone
- genug von etwas/jemandem haben

Füge die korrekte Verbform ein.
1. Little by little the rabbit became accustomed to me; at last I ... it out of my hand.
2. I ...n't ... the animals yet.
3. I am ... up with this business.

Übersetze:
1. Was gibst du deiner Katze zu fressen?
2. Sie zog es vor, ihr Baby zu stillen.
3. Er füttert die Katze nicht regelmäßig.

feel	felt	felt	(sich) (an)fühlen

Folgende Redewendungen solltest du lernen:
to feel like doing something
   - Lust haben, etwas zu tun
to feel one's way
   - sich vorwärts tasten; vorsichtig vorgehen

Füge die korrekte Verbform ein.
1. She ... out of place at their party.
2. I ... it my duty to help her.

Übersetze:
1. Ich habe mich noch nie so traurig gefühlt wie heute.
2. Ich habe Lust spazierenzugehen. Möchtest du
   mitkommen?

fight	fought	fought	(be)kämpfen

Folgende Redewendungen solltest du lernen:
to fight back one's tears
   - Tränen unterdrücken
to fight tooth and nail to do something
   - mit aller Kraft um etwas kämpfen

Füge die korrekte Verbform ein.
1. Rivals don't use ... duels any more.
2. He ... for his life.

Übersetze:
1. Sie haben jahrelang für ihre Unabhängigkeit gekämpft.
2. Sie kämpfte mit aller Kraft für eine Ausreiseerlaubnis.

find	found	found	finden

Füge die korrekte Verbform ein.
1. I ... it very difficult to go through this book.
2. Look, what I ... !

Übersetze:
1. Sie gruben in ihrem Garten, bis sie den Schatz fanden.

flee	fled	fled	fliehen

Füge die korrekte Verbform ein.
1. He ... the country because he feared that his fraud (Be-trug) might be discovered.
2. I haven't seen him since he ... .

Übersetze:
1. Die Feinde flohen als unsere Armee am Horizont auf-tauchte.
2. Ich habe nicht den geringsten Respekt vor ihr, denn sie flieht jede Gefahr.

fly	flew	flown	fliegen

Folgende Redewendungen solltest du lernen:
to fly high
   - ehrgeizig sein; hochgesteckte Ziele haben; hoch hinaus-
    wollen
to fly at someone
   - auf jemanden losgehen
to fly off the handle
   - aus der Haut fahren

Füge die korrekte Verbform ein.

1. How time ... !
2. I ... never ... on a plane in all my life.
3. When he heard about his daughter's last prank, he ... off the handle.
4. We ... from Djakarta to London by plane.

Übersetze:
1. Wir flogen über den Atlantik.
2. Sobald sie mich sah, flog sie in meine Arme.
3. Sieh wie spät es ist. Wir müssen schleunigst weg!
4. Die Tür flog auf, und Tom kam herein.

Beachte: Man darf dieses Verb nicht verwechseln mit 'flow/flowed/flowed' - fließen

Test 3: Setze alle korrekten Verbformen ein *(deal, dig, dive, draw, drink, drive, eat, fall, feed, feel, fight, find, flee, fly):*
1. We lost the thief out of sight when he ... into the crowd at Times Square.
2. He ... his own grave when he stole money out of the safe.
3. She ... high and I'm sure she will succeed.
4. The prices for cars ... tremendously.
5. She ... all night long.
6. I ... with him for almost ten years.
7. You ...n't yet ... up your meal, have you?
8. You shouldn't ... this meat to your dog!
9. I can't see what you ... at.
10. I ... him very attractive.
11. He ... very sorry for her when he heard about her misfortune.
12. Last year I ... my kite many times.
13. The government hasn't ... poverty yet.
14. The windows ... open because of the heavy storm.
15. He ... the curtains and fell asleep immediately.

Übersetze:
1. Bis jetzt haben wir nur Hüte verkauft (to deal with), doch nun verkaufen wir auch Spazierstöcke.
2. Bist du schon mal im Pazifik getaucht (dive)?
3. Ich hätte diese Szene zeichnen sollen (draw)!
4. Sie trinkt seit ihrer frühen Jugend (drink).
5. Es war sehr spät, als wir von der Party nach Hause fuhren (drive).
6. Früher gingen sie oft essen (eat).
7. Ich erschrak so sehr, daß ich die brennende Kerze fallenließ (fall).
8. Er ging nach Hause weil er sich krank fühlte (feel).
9. Sie war so traurig, daß sie die Tränen nicht unterdrücken konnte (feel).
10. Ich bin vor der Polizei geflohen (flee).
11. Der Vogel hat sich den Flügel gebrochen und nun kann er nicht mehr fliegen.
12. Ich bin noch nie zuvor mit dieser Fluglinie geflogen.

forbid	forbade	forbidden	verbieten

Folgende Redewendung solltest du lernen:
God forbid that
  - Gott mögen uns davor behüten, daß

Füge die korrekte Verbform ein.
1. The teacher ... us to use that word.
2. In this country it is ... to drink in public.
3. His parents ... him to marry that girl.

Übersetze:
1. Gott möge uns davor behüten, daß er zurückkommt.
2. Er verbat uns, das Haus zu verlassen, solange der Sturm andauerte.
3. Er ist in diesem Geschäft verboten, die Ware anzufassen.

Hinweis: forbidding - abstoßend, widerwärtig, bedrohlich

forget	forgot	forgotten	vergessen

Folgende Redewendungen solltest du lernen:
to forget oneself
  - sich vergessen; aus der Rolle fallen
Forget it!
  - Vergiß es! Es ist nicht wichtig!
Forget about it!
  - Reg dich nicht auf!

Füge die korrekte Verbform ein.
1. He ... to lock the door.
2. I'm afraid I ... to turn off the lights; they are still burning.
3. Don't ... to call me before noon.
4. I ... you.
5. ... you ... me?
6. Where ... you ... your gloves?

Übersetze:
1. Sie vergaß immer etwas bei mir.
2. Ich habe all mein Französisch verlernt.
3. Ich habe meinen Koffer im Zug vergessen.

forgave	forgiven	vergeben, vergessen

Folgende Redewendung solltest du lernen:
to forgive someone a debt
  - jemandem eine Schuld erlassen

Füge die korrekte Verbform ein.
1. As I apologized, she ... me.
2. Please, ... me for not having called you.
3. She never ... anybody.
4. I won't ... you that.

Übersetze:
1. Als wir nicht zahlen konnten, hat sie uns unsere Schuld erlassen.
2. Er sagte, er würde mir nie vergeben.
3. Sie war froh, daß wir ihr vergaben.

freeze	froze	frozen	(ge)frieren

Folgende Redewendungen solltest du lernen:
to freeze in one's tracks
  - wie angewurzelt stehenbleiben
to freeze someone to the spot
  - wie angewurzelt stehenbleiben wegen etwas
to make someone's blood freeze
  - jemandes Blut in den Adern erstarren lassen (vor Angst, Schreck)
to freeze to death
  - erfrieren

Füge die korrekte Verbform ein.
1. When she saw her double, she ... in her tracks.
2. The sight of her ... me on the spot.
3. The prisoners were so badly looked after that they ... to death.

Übersetze:
1. Der See war zugefroren .
2. Die Erscheinung des Geistes ließ ihr das Blut in den Adern erstarren.
3. Sie fanden den Weg zurück nicht und erfroren.
4. Friere das übriggebliebene Essen doch einfach ein!

| get | got | got | bekommen, werden |

Folgende Redewendungen solltest du lernen:
to get something across
   - etwas „rüberbringen"; etwas verständlich machen
to get into a jam
   - in Schwierigkeiten geraten
to get down to business
   - zur Sache kommen
to get along with someone
   - mit jemandem auskommen
to get carried away
   - sich mitreißen lassen
to get in touch with someone
   - mit jemandem Kontakt aufnehmen; jemanden anrufen
to get out of hand
   - außer Kontrolle geraten
to get rid of something/someone
   - etwas/jemanden loswerden
to get the better of something
   - etwas überwinden
to get on someone's nerves
   - jemandem auf die Nerven gehen
to get away with something
   - ungestraft davonkommen mit etwas
to get the sack
   - entlassen werden
to get something over with
   - etwas hinter sich bringen
How are you? - Well, I get by. - Wie geht's?
   - Es geht so; ich komme so zurecht.
What has got into you?
   - Was ist denn in dich gefahren?

Füge die korrekte Verbform ein.
1. In the course of time they ... to know him better.
2. I have ... the flue, so be careful!
3. It's useless, I just don't ... along with him.
4. I ... the better of my fear and mounted on the plane.

Übersetze:
1. Was hast du da?
2. Sieh, was ich von meinen Eltern bekommen habe!

3. Du wirst mit ihr auskommen müssen, ob du möchtest oder nicht!
4. Du siehst so ärgerlich aus. Was ist in dich gefahren?
5. Los, laß uns dieses Gespräch hinter uns bringen.
6. Um Mitternacht war er immer noch hier. Ich konnte ihn einfach nicht loswerden.

| give | gave | given | geben |

Folgende Redewendungen solltest du lernen:
to give someone the cold shoulder
- jemandem die kalte Schulter zeigen
to give rise to
- verursachen
to give someone one's love
- jemandem herzliche Grüße bestellen von sich
to give in to someone
- jemandem nachgeben
to give someone a hand with something
- jemandem bei etwas helfen
to give evidence of something
- zeugen von etwas
to give birth to
- gebären; zur Welt bringen
to give way to something
- Platz machen für etwas; ersetzt werden durch
to give something (a secret) away
- etwas verraten, ausplaudern
Don't give me that!
- Das glaubst du doch selbst nicht!
I don't give a damn about it!
- Das ist mir völlig egal!
to give someone a piece of one's mind
- jemandem ordentlich die Meinung sagen
to give a smile to someone
- jemanden anlächeln
to give a lecture
- einen Vortrag halten
to give the world for something
- alles geben für etwas

Füge die korrekte Verbform ein.
1. Little by little his anger ... way to comprehension.
2. The professor ... a lecture on Nabokov.
3. I ...n't yet ... up the hope of seeing him again.
4. You could have succeeded. Why did you ... up so soon?

Übersetze:
1. Du hast einfach zu schnell aufgegeben. Du hättest dich ein bißchen mehr anstrengen müssen!
2. Ich gebe dir das Buch, sobald ich es gelesen habe.
3. Sie lächelte mich an und verschwand.
4. Vergiß nicht, du hast mir dein Wort gegeben, niemandem etwas zu sagen.
5. Wieviel Geld habe ich dir bis jetzt gegeben?

go	went	gone	gehen (fahren, reisen)

Folgende Redewendungen solltest du lernen:
to go to the dogs
   - vor die Hunde gehen
to go by appearances
   - nach dem Aussehen urteilen
to go out of one's way to do something
   - sich besondere Mühe geben bei etwas
to go off the beaten track
   - etwas Ungewöhnliches tun
to go for a walk
   - spazieren gehen
to go to great troubles/lengths to do something
   - sich besondere Mühe geben bei etwas
to go on and on about something
   - nicht aufhören, über etwas zu reden
to go with the times
   - mit der Zeit gehen
to go too far
   - zu weit gehen
There you go!
   - Na also!
That goes for all of you!
   - Das gilt für euch alle!
That goes without saying.
   - Das versteht sich von selbst.

Füge die korrekte Verbform ein.
1. I ... out in search of some firewood.
2. They probably ... out for a walk since they don't answer the bell.
3. This time you ... too far!
4. Last year he ... through a serious illness.
5. Where did you ... last summer?
6. Are you ... already?
7. It seems he never ... to school.
8. You shouldn't ... to meet him at that place!
9. Do you know where he ... to?
10. They ... to Switzerland last winter.
11. On Sundays we always ... to the cinema.

Übersetze:
1. Er hörte nicht auf, über seine Operation zu reden.
2. Unser König sagte immer man müsse mit der Zeit gehen.
3. Weißt du, welche dieser Straßen nach Bath führt?
4. Ich bin rein zufällig dorthin gegangen.

Test 4: Setze alle korrekten Verbformen ein *(forbid, forget, freeze, get, give, go):*
1. I ... the sack, so I'll have to look for a new job.
2. ... about your troubles and come and join us.
3. I ... you to leave.
4. We are ... the use of the elevator.
5. You should ... her that.
6. I'm glad you never ... me anything!
7. A language is easily ... .
8. I ... already ... you some advice, haven't I?
9. I'm glad he ... me all my faults.
10. Are you sure it is all ... and forgotten?
11. I ... you for having been so rude to him.
12. In all this time, she hasn't ... me my impertinence.
13. Don't you think it is time to ... us?
14. Don't go skating on this lake. It isn't yet thoroughly ... over.
15. He ... to hand me back my keys.
16. She hasn't turned up yet. I'm afraid she ... our rendez-vous.
17. The heating didn't work and I was ... .
18. Where did you ... this beautiful hat?
19. I don't think he really ... her.
20. I should ... her a piece of advice.

Übersetze:
1. Der Kellner ist wütend, weil ein Gast vergessen hat zu zahlen (forget).
2. Ich habe vergessen, eine Reservierung im Restaurant zu machen (forget).
3. Bitte vergib mir dafür, daß ich so wenig freundlich zu dir war (forgive).
4. Hast du mir vergeben (forgive)?
5. Du hättest ihr nie vergeben sollen (forgive)!
6. Sie konnten den Boden nicht aufgraben weil er gefroren war (freeze).
7. Ich habe deinen Brief noch nicht bekommen (get).
8. Diese Band hat noch nie ein Konzert gegeben (give).
9. Ich muß sie anrufen. Weißt du, wo sie hingegangen ist (go)?

grow	grew	grown	wachsen

Folgende Redewendungen solltest du lernen:
to grow old/dark /...
  - alt/dunkel /... werden
to grow apart
  - sich auseinander entwickeln; sich auseinander leben
to grow in wisdom
  - weiser werden

Füge die korrekte Verbform ein.

1. Suddenly I realized how old he ... .
2. We tried ... tomatoes in our garden but it wouldn't work.
3. He thought he ... in wisdom but I tell you this was an illusion.

Übersetze:
1. Du bist gar nicht gewachsen, seit ich dich das letzte Mal gesehen habe.
2. Sieh, wie sehr mein Haar gewachsen ist!
3. Der Boden ist sehr viel dunkler geworden, seit wir den Teppich weggenommen haben.

hang	hung	hung	hängen

Folgende Redewendung solltest du lernen:
to let something go hang
   - etwas vernachlässigen; sich nicht scheren um etwas

Füge die korrekte Verbform ein.
1. Did you see how he ... on her lips?
2. I ... just ... the picture you painted on the wall.
3. I think this lamp ... too low. You will hurt your head!

Übersetze:
1. Hast du die Wäsche schon aufgehängt?
2. Kein einziges Bild hing an seiner Wand.

Beachte: „hang" wird regelmäßig gebildet bei:

The murderer was hanged
   - Der Mörder wurde gehängt

have	had	had	haben

Folgende Redewendungen solltest du lernen:
to have a good command of something
   - etwas beherrschen; gut können
to have a go at something
   - etwas ausprobieren, versuchen
to have a crush on someone
   - in jemanden verknallt sein
to have a grudge against someone
   - jemandem grollen
to have a liking for someone
   - jemanden gern mögen; eine Vorliebe haben für
    jemanden
to have a word with someone
   - kurz mit jemandem sprechen
to have what it takes
   - das gewisse Etwas haben; das Zeug haben zu
to have one's heart in one's mouth
   - zu Tode erschrocken sein
to have one's way
   - seinen Willen/Kopf durchsetzen

to have the time of one's life
  - einen Riesenspaß haben
I had better do it
  - ich sollte es besser tun; es wäre besser, wenn ich es täte

Füge die korrekte Verbform ein.
1. I ...n't ... breakfast yet.
2. Last week I ... a terrible cold so I didn't go to work.
3. He ... a surprisingly good command of German although he's never been to Germany.
4. I ... no doubt that he was telling the truth so I trusted him.
5. I ...n't many friends in my youth.
6. Yesterday we ... pizza for dinner.
7. I bet she's in love. She ... that special look in her eyes.

Übersetze:
1. Ich habe noch keine Nachricht von ihr erhalten, seit sie weggefahren ist.
2. Er hat ein extrem schlechtes Gedächtnis.
3. Du kannst diese Jacke haben, wenn dir kalt ist.
4. Ich hatte gestern Nacht einen merkwürdigen Traum.
5. Wir hatten eine dieser endlosen Diskussionen, die zu nichts führen.

hear	heard	heard	hören

Folgende Redewendung solltest du lernen:
to hear someone out
  - jemanden ausreden lassen

Füge die korrekte Verbform ein.
1. ... you ever ... that before?
2. I ...n't ... the bell ring.

Übersetze:
1. Da war ein Geräusch. Ich habe es genau gehört!
2. Sie ließ mich nie ausreden.

hide	hid	hidden	(sich) verstecken

Füge die korrekte Verbform ein.
1. She ... behind the door to frighten me.
2. He ... the money in a place he thought safe.

Übersetze:
1. Es gelang ihm nie, seine Gefühle zu verbergen.
2. Mir scheint, du hast etwas zu verbergen. Habe ich recht?

hit	hit	hit	schlagen, treffen

Folgende Redewendungen solltest du lernen:
to hit the nail on the head
    - den Nagel auf den Kopf treffen
to hit the jackpot
    - das große Los ziehen; Glück haben
to hit someone a blow
    - jemandem einen Schlag versetzen

Füge die korrekte Verbform ein.
1. Don't you ever ... me again.
2. Before she left, she ... him across the face.

Übersetze:
1. Mit seiner Bemerkung hat er den Nagel auf den Kopf
   getroffen.

hold	held	held	halten

Folgende Redewendungen solltest du lernen:
to hold one's nose/ears
    - sich die Nase/Ohren zuhalten
to hold on to something
    - festhalten an etwas (vgl. hang onto)
to hold one's breath
    - den Atem anhalten
to hold something back
    - etwas verschweigen; vorenthalten
to hold the view that
    - der Ansicht sein, daß

Füge die korrekte Verbform ein.
1. Please, ... the line (bleiben Sie am Apparat), I will get Mrs. Scott for you!
2. I'm sure this rain will not ... for long.
3. The child ... a bunch of flowers in its hands.

Übersetze:
1. Sie wirkt nervös. Ich bin sicher, daß sie uns etwas verschweigt.
2. Ich bin der Ansicht, daß Löwen nicht gejagt werden dürfen.

hurt	hurt	hurt	(sich) verletzen, wehtun

Folgende Redewendungen solltest du lernen:
He would not hurt a fly.
   - Er würde keiner Fliege etwas zuleide tun.
to hurt someone's feelings
   - jemandes Gefühle verletzen; jemanden kränken

Füge die korrekte Verbform ein.
1. You ... me very much when you criticized my work.
2. I'm afraid you ... her feelings.
3. She was badly ... in the accident.
4. You ...n't ... yourself, have you?

Übersetze:
1. Ich hoffe, du hast dich nicht verletzt.
2. Diese Schuhe haben mir von Anfang an wehgetan.
3. Du hast ihn mit deinem dummen Verhalten gekränkt.

keep	kept	kept	(be)halten, aufbewahren

Folgende Redewendungen solltest du lernen:
to keep something in mind
   - etwas nicht vergessen; an etwas denken
to keep in touch with someone
   - in Kontakt bleiben mit jemandem
to keep on doing something
   - etwas weiterhin tun; fortfahren, etwas zu tun

to keep someone company
  - jemandem Gesellschaft leisten
to keep up with someone
  - mit jemandem mithalten
Keep it up!
  - Weiter so!
to keep someone from doing something
  - jemanden davon abhalten, etwas zu tun
to keep up appearances
  - den Schein wahren
to keep someone waiting
  - jemanden warten lassen
to keep someone in the dark about something
  - jemanden über etwas im Ungewissen lassen
to keep cool
  - gelassen bleiben
to keep fit
  - fit; in Form bleiben
I won't keep you long
  - ich werde dich nicht lange aufhalten

Füge die korrekte Verbform ein.
1. I didn't mean you to ... this book!
2. I told him to calm down but he just ... screaming.
3. She ... me in the dark about this plan on purpose.
4. He told me he wouldn't ... me long but he did.
5. Look, I ... this photograph of yours you once gave me.
6. He never ... in touch with friends who would move away.
7. She ... her secret beyond the grave.

Übersetze:
1. Sie kamen zusammen zur Dinnerparty, um den Schein zu wahren.
2. Versuche bitte, an unsere Verabredung am Montag zu denken.
3. Ich war erstaunt, wie gelassen er blieb.
4. Er ist fit geblieben, indem er jeden Tag joggt.
5. Ich hoffe, es macht dir nichts, daß ich das Buch so lange behalten habe.

know	knew	known	kennen, wissen

Füge die korrekte Verbform ein.
1. I think I ... him once.
2. I ... this ever since you told me about it.
3. I told you I ... she wouldn't come.

Übersetze:
1. Ich wußte, daß unser Plan schiefgehen würde.
2. Sie wußte, daß sie ihn wiedersehen würde.

lay	laid	laid	legen

Füge die korrekte Verbform ein.
1. Mrs. Jones ... a mouse trap in her basement.
2. We ... down a huge blanket and enjoyed the sun.

Übersetze:
1. Danny hat den Tisch gedeckt.
2. Ich weiß nicht, wo ich meinen Hut hingelegt habe.
3. Hühner legen Eier.
4. Wo hat sie die Zeitung hingelegt?

lead	led	led	führen, leiten

Folgende Redewendungen solltest du lernen:
to lead someone astray
   - auf den falschen Weg führen; fehlleiten; vom richtigen
     Weg wegführen
to lead the way
   - den Weg zeigen; vorangehen
to lead up to
   - führen zu

Füge die korrekte Verbform ein.
1. He ... us through the city.
2. He ... her to believe that he was a multimillionaire.

Übersetze:
1. Ich war sicher, daß das zu einem Streit führen würde.
2. Die Straße, die wir nahmen, führte nach Edinburgh.

leap	lept/leaped	lept/leaped	springen (über)

Füge die korrekte Verbform ein.
1. He ... at her unexpected offer.
2. We ... the wall and entered the graveyard.

Übersetze:
1. Der Hund tat mir weh, als er an mir hochsprang.
2. Sie sprang ohne irgendeine Veranlassung in den See.

leave	left	left	(ver)lassen

Folgende Redewendungen solltest du lernen:
to leave it at that
   - es dabei belassen, bewenden lassen
to leave for Edinburgh
   - nach Edinburgh aufbrechen

Füge die korrekte Verbform ein.
1. I ... Tokyo a year ago.
2. How much money is there ... on your bank account?

Übersetze:
1. Sie sind gestern abend nach Frankreich aufgebrochen.
2. Sie hat mich für einen jüngeren Mann verlassen.
3. Ich dachte, du hättest deinen Mann schon längst verlassen.

lend	lent	lent	(ver)leihen

Folgende Redewendung solltest du lernen:
to lend an ear to someone
   - jemandem Gehör schenken

Füge die korrekte Verbform ein.
1. My parents ... me their car.
2. She ... me a large sum of money.

Übersetze:
1. Wieviel Geld hast du ihm geliehen?
2. Ist das dein Auto? - Nein, David hat es mir geliehen.

Folgende Redewendungen solltest du lernen:
to let oneself go
  - sich gehen lassen; aus sich herausgehen
to let someone down
  - jemanden im Stich lassen, enttäuschen
to let someone off
  - jemanden laufenlassen, davonkommen lassen
to let a room
  - ein Zimmer vermieten
let alone
  - geschweige denn
to let drop a remark
  - eine Bemerkung fallenlassen

Füge die korrekte Verbform ein.
1. They ... me the room for 30 pounds a week.
2. He felt really embarrassed for having ... himself go.
3. He ... me know that he would come home for Christmas.

Übersetze:
1. Laß uns schwimmen gehen!
2. Sie ließ mich wissen, daß sie nicht kommen würde.
3. Mein Freund ließ mich immer seine Hüte tragen.

| lie | lay | lain | liegen |

Folgende Redewendungen solltest du lernen:
to lie under an obligation
  - eine Verpflichtung haben
to lie in
  - ausschlafen; lange im Bett bleiben

Füge die korrekte Verbform ein.
1. The troops ... in ambush for the enemy.
2. She felt sick and had to ... down.
3. This burden ... heavily on me.

Übersetze:
1. Die alte Burg lag in Trümmern.
2. Der Schnee lag schwer auf den Ästen der Bäume.

Achtung: Das Verb „lie" kann man leicht verwechseln mit:

lie	lied	lied	lügen (regelm.)
lay	laid	laid	legen (s.o.)

Test 5: Setze alle korrekten Verbformen ein *(grow, hang, have, hear, hide, hit, hold, hurt, keep, know, lay, lead, leap, leave, lend, let, lie):*

1. You'll have to admit that we ... apart in the course of the years.
2. I ...n't from you for such a long time!
3. I let my studies go ... during the summer term.
4. Don't you see he ... a crush on you?
5. As it ... dark we decided to return home.
6. I ... a strange noise in the attic last night.
7. I'm sure he ... the money somewhere in the garden.
8. She ... her jewels somewhere and now she couldn't find them any more.
9. He was ... by a car as he stepped out headlessly into Piccadilly.
10. I ... my breath so that they wouldn't realize that I was in the room.
11. Take care not to ... yourself with that knife.
12. I fell down the stairs and ... my head.
13. We ... at the chance and left immediately for California.
14. She ... me see what she had written.
15. Once we ... a dog.
16. He ... without saying good-bye.
17. He ... a choir in his early youth.
18. I am very glad she ... her promise.
19. The children had been ... in bed all day long.
20. I ... my head against the wall as I stumbled.
21. I'm afraid there is nothing ... over.
22. I know I ... you the book but now I want it back.
23. I assure you that I ... the text by heart just a moment ago.
24. By the time I left New York I ... the city inside out.
25. It's amazing how he always manages ... it his way.
26. She ... me company until I had to leave for the train.
27. Do you know where I ... my bag?
28. I ... this pie for you.
29. Their quarrel ... up to a divorce.
30. I'm glad you ... me an ear.
31. London ... on the River Thames.
32. His work ... a lot to be desired but we accepted it nevertheless.

| light | lit/lighted | lit/lighted | anzünden, beleuchten |

Folgende Redewendungen solltest du lernen:
to light upon something
   - landen auf etwas; etwas durch Zufall entdecken
to be lit up
   - angeheitert sein; beschwipst sein

Füge die korrekte Verbform ein.
1. She ... a cigarette and sat down.
2. Her eyes ... up when she saw him enter the room.

Übersetze:
1. Das Zimmer war ausschließlich von Kerzen erleuchtet.
2. Seine Augen leuchteten auf, als ich ihm erzählte, daß
   sie zurückgekommen sei.

| lose | lost | lost | verlieren |

Folgende Redewendungen solltest du lernen:
to lose the thread (of one's argument)
   - den Faden verlieren
to lose one's mind
   - verrückt werden
to lose one's temper
   - die Geduld verlieren, wütend werden
to lose touch with someone
   - den Kontakt mit jemandem verlieren
to lose oneself in a book
   - sich in ein Buch vertiefen
to be lost in thought
   - in Gedanken verloren sein

Füge die korrekte Verbform ein.
1. How can he behave this way? It seems he ... his mind!
2. I can't tell you what she's doing because I ... touch
   with her.

Übersetze:
1. Wir haben all unser Geld beim Pferderennen verloren.
2. Ich bin froh zu sehen, daß du dein Selbstvertrauen nicht
   verloren hast.

3. Ich habe Angst, meinem Hauswirt zu sagen, daß ich die Schlüssel verloren habe.

make	made	made	machen, tun

Folgende Redewendungen solltest du lernen:
to make someone do something
- jemanden veranlassen, etwas zu tun; jemanden etwas tun lassen

to make a fuss about something
- viel Aufhebens von etwas machen

to make something up
- etwas erfinden; sich etwas ausdenken

to make up for something
- etwas wiedergutmachen

to make up one's mind
- sich entschließen; eine Entscheidung treffen

to make for the door
- auf die Tür zusteuern, zueilen

to make sense of something
- etwas verstehen, begreifen

to make both ends meet
- über die Runden kommen, sich nach der Decke strecken

Füge die korrekte Verbform ein.
1. She forced me to drink this terrible tea she ... .
2. You ... me love you.
3. ... you ... up your mind by now?
4. He ... up for having behaved so cruelly by sending me a bunch of flowers.
5. She ... a terrible fuss about this silly matter.
6. I don't believe a word of what she said. I'm sure she ... up all of it.

Übersetze:
1. Ich habe einen Kuchen für die Party heute abend gemacht.
2. Warte einen Augenblick, ich habe noch keinen Kaffee gemacht.
3. Sie machte sich eine Tasse Tee und setzte sich auf das Sofa.
4. Er machte es sich auf dem Sofa bequem.

5. Als sie merkte, wie spät es war, sprang sie auf und eilte auf die Tür zu.
6. Er ließ sie glauben, er sei nicht im geringsten interessiert.
7. Er hat keinen guten Eindruck auf mich gemacht.
8. Ich habe einen dummen Fehler gemacht.
9. Der Clown machte uns lachen.

mean	meant	meant	meinen, bedeuten

Füge die korrekte Verbform ein.
1. We were ... to meet.
2. Is this ... to be a joke?

Übersetze:
1. Es tut mir leid, ich wollte dich nicht stören.
2. Bist du sicher, daß ihre Bemerkung ein Witz sein sollte?

meet	met	met	begegnen, treffen

Folgende Redewendungen solltest du lernen:
to meet with approval
  - Beifall finden
to meet with a refusal
  - auf Ablehnung stoßen

Füge die korrekte Verbform ein.
1. We ... last night at the theatre.
2. Didn't I tell you that John and I ... last summer?

Übersetze:
1. Mein Vorschlag stieß leider auf Ablehnung.
2. Wir haben uns zufällig in New York getroffen.

pay	paid	paid	(be)zahlen

Folgende Redewendung solltest du lernen:
to pay someone a visit
  - jemanden besuchen

Füge die korrekte Verbform ein.
1. I ...n't ... the bill yet.
2. She never ... attention to what I was saying.

Übersetze:
1. Er machte ihr nie Komplimente.
2. Wir haben unser Haus letztes Jahr endlich abbezahlt.
3. Er zahlte seine Schulden nie zurück.

put	put	put	setzen, stellen, legen

Folgende Redewendungen solltest du lernen:
to put on an act
   - Theater spielen; sich verstellen
to put into words
   - in Worte fassen
to put one's foot in
   - ins Fettnäpfchen treten
to put an end to something
   - etwas ein Ende bereiten
to put something right
   - etwas richtigstellen
to put the blame for something on someone
   - jemandem die Schuld für etwas geben
to put up with something
   - sich etwas gefallen lassen; sich abfinden mit etwas
to put into action/practice
   - in die Tat umsetzen
to put something off
   - etwas aufschieben, verschieben
to put on weight
   - zunehmen (Gewicht)
to put someone in his place
   - jemanden in seine Schranken weisen
to put the cart before the horse
   - das Pferd von hinten aufzäumen
to put one's foot down
   - ein Machtwort sprechen; energisch werden; einschreiten

Füge die korrekte Verbform ein.
1. Why did you ... on a jeans to your sister's wedding? It would have been more decent to wear a suit!

2. I can't find the tea-pot. Where ... you ... it?
3. ... you ... sugar in my tea?
4. The police finally ... an end to bootlegging.
5. ... you ... out the light in the kitchen?
6. You really ... your foot in! Now let's hope she won't be angry for too long.

Übersetze:
1. Suchst du die Schlüssel? Ich habe sie auf den Tisch gelegt.
2. Sie legte die Füße auf den Tisch und schaltete den Fernseher ein.
3. Hast du deinen Regenmantel angezogen?
4. Ich habe das Essen, das übriggeblieben ist, in den Kühlschrank gestellt.

Test 6: *Setze alle korrekten Verbformen ein (light, lose, make, mean, meet, pay, put):*

1. We ... a lot of money for this television set.
2. She put on some music and ... the candles.
3. He ... his temper because I was late again.
4. I assure you that I ... you no harm!
5. Don't pass this street at night. It is very badly ... .
6. He ... sure that I would be invited to the party.
7. You're not ... to answer the phone!
8. ... you ... on your coat?
9. The first time I went to Los Angeles, I got completely ... .
10. We ... in London and went to Bath together.
11. I was very pleased ... him.
12. Last time we ... we had a quarrel.
13. I ... him back some day!
14. Her new novel ... with great approval.
15. Mrs Smith ... me a visit yesterday and we had some tea together.
16. Imagine! Our street is ... by gas!
17. He ... dearly for his sins.
18. I'm afraid your favourite horse ... the race, Mr Smith! We have to leave!
19. I can't ... my feelings into words.

Übersetze:
1. Das Feuer im Kamin erleuchtete das ganze Zimmer (light).
2. Weißt du, ob er sein Bein im Krieg verloren hat (lose)?
3. Deine Liebe bedeutete mir viel (mean).
4. Ist dieses Geschenk für deine Großmutter gedacht (mean)?
5. Ich habe gerade meine Frau mit einem anderen Mann getroffen (meet).
6. Ich ziehe es vor, bar zu zahlen (pay).
7. Hast du deine Rechnungen schon bezahlt (pay)?
8. Wo hast du das Geld, das ich dir gegeben habe, hingetan (put)?

read	read	read	lesen

Folgende Redewendungen solltest du lernen:
to read between the lines
   - zwischen den Zeilen lesen
to read a subject at university
   - ein Fach studieren
to read on
   - weiterlesen
to read something out
   - etwas laut vorlesen
to read up on something
   - nachlesen über etwas
to take it as read that
   - davon ausgehen können, daß
to be well-read in something
   - belesen sein in etwas; viel wissen über etwas

Füge die korrekte Verbform ein.
1. I ... just ... quite an interesting article about whales in the newspaper.
2. You won't be able to sing in a choir as long as you can't ... music.

Übersetze:
1. Hast du schon den neuen Roman von Stephen King gelesen?
2. Hast du schon mal einen Roman von Hemingway gelesen?

ride	rode	ridden	reiten, fahren

Folgende Redewendungen solltest du lernen:
to ride on air
   - selig sein vor Glück; wie auf Wolken schweben
to ride high
   - ganz oben sein; viel Erfolg haben
to ride for a fall
   - eine riskante Sache machen
to be ridden by fears
   - angstgepeinigt sein

Füge die korrekte Verbform ein.
1. ... you ever ... a horse through Arizona?
2. He must be ... by the devil to act so foolishly.

Übersetze:
1. Bist du jemals auf einem Elefanten geritten?
2. Der Bandit erschoß seinen Rivalen und ritt auf einem Schimmel davon.

ring	rang	rung	läuten

Folgende Redewendungen solltest du lernen:
to ring someone up
   - jemanden anrufen
that rings a bell
   - das kommt mir bekannt vor; das erinnert mich an etwas
to ring hollow
   - hohl, unglaubwürdig klingen

Füge die korrekte Verbform ein.
1. Don't you think his excuse ... hollow?
2. I ... you up at least three times yesterday.
3. I ...n't yet ... back aunt Laurie.

Übersetze:
1. Kommt dir das nicht bekannt vor?
2. Ich glaube, jemand hat an der Tür geläutet.

rise	rose	risen	aufstehen, (auf)steigen

Folgende Redewendungen solltest du lernen:
to rise to the occasion
   - sich der Lage gewachsen zeigen
to rise (up) against someone
   - sich erheben gegen; rebellieren gegen
Rise and shine!
   - Aufstehen! Raus aus den Federn!

Füge die korrekte Verbform ein.
1. When I went to school, I used ... at 7 a.m.
2. The sun ... already; we've got to be going.

Übersetze:
1. Der Vorhang ging auf und die Schauspieler erschienen auf
   der Bühne.
2. Die Preise für Pelzmäntel sind in den letzten zehn
   Jahren beachtlich gestiegen.

Achtung: Wie „rise" wird gebildet: „arise/arose/arisen" - sich erheben.
Man darf „rise" nicht verwechseln mit:
„raise/raised/raised" - (er)heben.

run	ran	run	rennen, laufen

Folgende Redewendungen solltest du lernen:
to run across someone
   - jemandem zufällig begegnen; auf jemanden stoßen
to run out of something
   - etwas nicht mehr haben
to run someone over
   - jemanden überfahren
Still waters run deep.
   - Stille Wasser sind tief.

Füge die korrekte Verbform ein.
1. He was so scared that he ... all the way home.
2. Do you know where she ... to?

Übersetze:
1. Ich bin gelaufen, so schnell ich konnte.
2. Sie ist von zu Hause weggelaufen.
3. Er rannte über die Straße, um seinen Hund zu fangen.

say	said	said	sagen

Folgende Redewendungen solltest du lernen:
that is easier said than done
  - das ist leichter gesagt als getan
it goes without saying that
  - es versteht sich von selbst, daß
that is to say
  - das heißt; vielmehr
to say nothing of ...
  - ganz zu schweigen von ...

Füge die korrekte Verbform ein.
1. She ... she wouldn't come to our party.
2. O.k., you ... that already.
3. Did you understand what he ...?

Übersetze:
1. Er sagte, es sei nicht einfach gewesen, eine Einladung
   zu bekommen.
2. Ich habe kein einziges Wort von dem, was er gesagt hat,
   verstanden.
3. Es ist schwer zu sagen, wer gewinnen wird.
4. Sie wirkt verärgert. Was hast du zu ihr gesagt?

see	saw	seen	sehen

Folgende Redewendungen solltest du lernen:
to see no further than one's nose
  - engstirnig sein
to see about something
  - sich kümmern um etwas
to see how the wind blows
  - sehen, woher der Wind weht; die Lage abschätzen
to see someone home
  - jemanden nach Hause begleiten

to see someone off
  - jemanden verabschieden
to see someone out
  - jemanden hinausbegleiten
to see someone's point
  - verstehen, was jemand will, meint
to see something through
  - etwas zu Ende bringen
to see to it that
  - dafür sorgen, daß; darauf achten, daß
to live to see
  - etwas (noch) erleben
to see the sights
  - die Sehenswürdigkeiten besichtigen
to see red
  - rot sehen; wütend werden; in Wut geraten
to see for oneself
  - sich persönlich von etwas überzeugen
Seeing is believing.
  - Ich glaube nur, was ich mit eigenen Augen sehe.
to see eye to eye with someone
  - mit jemandem völlig übereinstimmen
to have seen better days
  - in einem schlechten Zustand sein; schon mal bessere
    Tage gesehen haben
to see the light
  - die Erleuchtung haben; verstehen; zur Einsicht kommen;
    entstehen; auftreten

Füge die korrekte Verbform ein.
1. When ... you ... him last?
2. I ... you the other day at the subway station.
3. What is Robin doing? I ...n't ... her for years!
4. Dave always ... me to the door.
5. I ... her running across the street.
6. She said she ... a green cat the other day.

Übersetze:
1. Ich habe ihn nur einmal gesehen.
2. Hast du den neuen Film von Saura schon gesehen?
3. Es war sehr nett von dir, mich nach Hause zu begleiten.
4. Hast du schon mal einen Bären gesehen?
5. Es war so neblig, daß wir nichts sehen konnten.

seek	sought	sought	(auf)suchen, versuchen

Folgende Redewendungen solltest du lernen:
to seek someone out
  - jemanden ausfindig machen; aufs Korn nehmen
to be much sought-after
  - sehr gefragt, begehrt sein

Füge die korrekte Verbform ein.

1. They ... safety in a doorway.
2. Well, I really ... to convince him.

Übersetze:
1. Diese Schreibmaschinen sind sehr gefragt.
2. Schließlich machten wir Onkel Toby in Hongkong ausfindig.

sell	sold	sold	verkaufen

Füge die korrekte Verbform ein.

1. This book is ... on the condition that it shall not be
   reprinted.
2. 30.000 copies ... been ... by now.

Übersetze:
1. Sie verkauften ihr Haus und ließen sich scheiden.
2. Das Theaterstück war innerhalb einer Stunde ausver-
   kauft.

send	sent	sent	senden, schicken

Folgende Redewendung solltest du lernen:
to send someone packing
  - jemanden fortjagen

Füge die korrekte Verbform ein.

1. He ...n't ... me his new adress yet.
2. She ... word to me that she wouldn't arrive before 9 p.m.

1. Die Eltern schickten ihre Kinder ins Bett und gingen ins Kino.
2. Hast du deinen Großeltern schon mal ein Telegramm geschickt?

set	set	set	setzen, stellen, legen

Folgende Redewendungen solltest du lernen:

to set someone free
- jemanden freilassen

to set out for
- aufbrechen, sich aufmachen nach

to set out on a journey
- eine Reise antreten

to set something on fire
- etwas anzünden

to set foot in
- eintreten

to set one's mind on something
- sich etwas in den Kopf setzen

to be dead set against something
- entschieden gegen etwas sein

to be set on doing something
- entschlossen sein, etwas zu tun

to set the alarm-clock
- den Wecker stellen

to set one's heart on something
- sein Herz an etwas hängen

to set the pace
- das Tempo angeben

to be all set for something
- fertig, vorbereitet für etwas sein; bereit, startklar sein

to set one's mind at rest
- sich beruhigen

to set eyes on something
- etwas zum ersten Mal sehen

to set out to do something
- sich vornehmen, etwas zu tun; sich an etwas machen

Füge die korrekte Verbform ein.
1. The teacher ... us a lot of homework.
2. ... you already ... the table?
3. She ... the broom aside and started screaming at me.
4. Where ... this novel ...?
5. They ... the flat on fire to destroy evidence.
6. You shouldn't ever ... all your hopes on her.

Übersetze:
1. Habt ihr euren neuen Kühlschrank schon aufgestellt?
2. Der Gefangene wurde erst letzte Woche freigelassen.
3. Sie treten ihre Weltreise nächste Woche an.
4. Sie hat sich in den Kopf gesetzt, nach Alaska zu gehen.
5. Ich bin entschieden gegen deinen dummen Plan.
6. Die Sonne ist noch nicht untergegangen.

| shake | shook | shaken | schütteln |

Folgende Redewendungen solltest du lernen:
to shake like a leaf
   - wie Espenlaub zittern
to be shaken by something
   - erschüttert sein über etwas
to shake someone up
   - jemanden aufrütteln

Füge die korrekte Verbform ein.
1. Take care not ...the can before opening it.
2. I got scared when the mean looking stranger ... his fist at me.
3. Nothing in the world could ever ... his faith in her.
4. He said no and ... his head.

Übersetze:
1. Warum hast du den Kopf geschüttelt?
2. Es gelang mir nicht, meinen Verfolger abzuschütteln.
3. Sie schüttelte mir niemals die Hand.

Folgende Redewendungen solltest du lernen:
to shed light on something
- Licht auf eine Sache werfen; zur Aufklärung von etwas beitragen
to shed new light on something
- neues Licht auf etwas werfen
to shed a bad habit
- eine schlechte Gewohnheit ablegen
to shed one's inhibitions
- seine Hemmungen ablegen
not shed any tears over someone
- jemandem keine Träne nachweinen
to shed their leaves
- ihre Blätter abwerfen (Bäume)

Füge die korrekte Verbform ein.
1. She ...n't ... any tears over the death of her husband.
2. This lamp ... so dim a light that you can hardly read.
3. The camp fire ...n't ... any warmth at all.

Übersetze:
1. Die andere Lampe hat ein angenehmeres Licht verbreitet.
2. Die meisten Bäume haben ihre Blätter noch nicht abgeworfen.

Test 7: *Füge die korrekte Verbform ein (read, ride, ring, rise, run, say, see, seek, sell, send, set, shake, shed):*

1. She never ... a word to me.
2. I think he ... my thoughts.
3. He ... away on a black horse.
4. ... you already ... for the room service?
5. When its father entered the room, the child ... from the floor to kiss him.
6. He was known for ... after women.
7. Do you know what subject she ... at university?
8. I ... across Anne yesterday.
9. I ... through the desert on a horse with no name.
10. Why ...n't you ... hands?

11. He ... early to go out fishing.
12. ... you ever ... a film by Billy Wilder?
13. Finally I managed to ... my old car but I ... it at a loss.
14. He says he ... me a letter but I never received it.
15. It was so hot they ... the shade.
16. The sun ... at 8.30 p.m. yesterday.
17. Too much blood ... in this war.
18. The moon ... a soft light on the park.

Übersetze:
1. Hast du den Brief gelesen, den ich dir geschrieben habe (read)?
2. Er ritt so schnell er konnte (ride).
3. Er wurde von einem Lastwagen überfahren (run).
4. Er sagte in seinem Brief, daß er uns im November besuchen würde (say).
5. Ich glaube, ich habe verstanden, was du meinst (see).
6. Ich habe meine Wohnung an einen reichen Mann verkauft (sell).
7. Wir haben unser Dienstmädchen letzten Donnerstag endlich fortgejagt (send).
8. Er hatte soviel Angst, daß er wie Espenlaub zitterte (shake).
9. Sie hat keine ihrer schlechten Gewohnheiten abgelegt (shed).

shine	shone	shone	scheinen, glänzen

Folgende Redewendung solltest du lernen:
to shine in/at something
   - in/bei etwas glänzen; herausragend sein in einer Sache

Füge die korrekte Verbform ein.
1. As the clouds moved away, the sun ... out.
2. Her long hair ... in the sun.
3. Did you notice how her eyes ... with happiness?

Übersetze:
1. Im Winter scheint die Sonne weniger als im Sommer.
2. Die Sonne schien gestern den ganzen Tag.
3. Raus aus den Federn!

shoot	shot	shot	(er)schießen

Folgende Redewendungen solltest du lernen:
to shoot ahead
   - schnelle Fortschritte machen
to have shot one's bolt
   - sein Pulver verschossen haben; keine Argumente mehr
    haben
to shoot questions at someone
   - jemanden mit Fragen bombardieren
to shoot the lights
   - bei Rot über die Kreuzung fahren
to shoot a glance at something
   - einen schnellen Blick werfen auf etwas
to shoot a photograph/film
   - ein Foto/einen Film machen
to shoot heroin
   - sich Heroin spritzen

Füge die korrekte Verbform ein.
1. He ... his rival with a gun.
2. Last year we ... a film in India.
3. She was ... by accident.

Übersetze:
1. Er warf einen Blick auf das Buch und legte es weg.
2. Sie hat ziemlich viele Fotos in Nepal gemacht.
3. Diese Szene mußten wir mehr als zehnmal drehen.

show	showed	shown	zeigen

Folgende Redewendungen solltest du lernen:
to show someone in
   - jemanden hereinführen
to show someone round
   - jemanden herumführen
to show up
   - aufkreuzen; erscheinen
to show someone around the town
   - jemandem die Stadt zeigen
to show one's hand/cards
   - seine Karten offen auf den Tisch legen, aufdecken

Füge die korrekte Verbform ein.
1. They ... us round Manhattan.
2. ... I ... this to you yet?
3. They didn't ask us to ... our invitation.

Übersetze:
1. Wie oft habe ich dir schon gezeigt, wie man Eier kocht!
2. Ich verstehe nicht, warum sie noch nicht aufgekreuzt ist!
3. Sie zeigte nie ihre Gefühle.

shrink	shrank	shrunk	einschrumpfen; einlaufen

Folgende Redewendungen solltest du lernen:
to shrink (back) from something
  - zurückschrecken vor etwas
to shrink into oneself
  - sich in sich selbst zurückziehen

Füge die korrekte Verbform ein.
1. My jeans ... so I can't wear them any more.
2. He ... back from singing in public.

Übersetze:
1. Sobald man ihn kritisiert, zieht er sich in sich selbst
   zurück.
2. Dieses Hemd war früher nicht so eng; ich bin sicher, daß
   es eingegangen ist.

Beachte: Adjektivisch wird manchmal „shrunken" verwendet:
a shrunken head, shrunken cheeks
- abgemagert, eingefallen

shut	shut	shut	schließen, zumachen

Folgende Redewendungen solltest du lernen:
Shut up!
  - Halt den Mund! Sei still!
to shut one's eyes to something
  - die Augen vor etwas verschließen
to keep one's mouth shut
  - den Mund halten; schweigen

Füge die korrekte Verbform ein.
1. She ... her eyes and fell asleep immediately.
2. You ...n't ... the door properly.
3. There is a terrible draught! Why don't you ... one of the windows?

Übersetze:
1. Sie schloß die Tür weil sie fror.
2. Er schloß die Augen und stellte sich vor, an einem Palmenstrand zu liegen.

sing	sang	sung	singen

Folgende Redewendungen solltest du lernen:
to sing another song/tune
  - einen anderen Ton anschlagen
to sing small/low
  - klein beigeben; kleinlaut werden
to sing someone to sleep
  - jemanden in den Schlaf singen

Füge die korrekte Verbform ein.
1. He always ... while taking his shower.
2. She ... her child to sleep.
3. He ... to me all evening.

Übersetze:
1. Hat dich deine Mutter nie in den Schlaf gesungen?
2. Er hat gestern im Konzert ziemlich viele schöne Lieder gesungen.
3. Habt ihr dieses Jahr Weihnachtslieder gesungen?
4. Wir hatten einmal einen Papagei, der ständig „Love me tender" sang.

sink	sank	sunk	(ver)sinken, (ver)senken

Folgende Redewendungen solltest du lernen:
to sink into oblivion
  - in Vergessenheit geraten
to sink into sleep
  - in tiefen Schlaf fallen

to sink into grief
 - in Kummer versinken
someone's heart sinks into his boots
 - jemandem rutscht das Herz in die Hose

Füge die korrekte Verbform ein.
1. The ship ... near the Spanish coast.
2. His compositions soon ... into oblivion.
3. The prices ... slightly during the last few days.

Übersetze:
1. Nach dem Tod seiner Frau versank er in tiefen Kummer.
2. Er sank auf das Sofa und schlief ein.
3. Ich dachte, dieses Schiff wäre versunken!

sit	sat	sat	sitzen

Folgende Redewendungen solltest du lernen:
to sit back and do nothing
 - die Hände in den Schoß legen
to sit on one's hands
 - keinen Finger rühren
to sit on the fence
 - zwischen zwei Stühlen sitzen
to sit up for someone
 - für jemanden aufbleiben; auf jemanden warten

Füge die korrekte Verbform ein.
1. My mother used to ... up for me every time I went dancing.
2. We ... down and had a drink.
3. Why don't you just ... down and relax?

Übersetze:
1. Sie setzte sich in einen Lehnstuhl und begann, ein Buch zu lesen.
2. Sie saßen alle am Tisch und warteten nur auf mich.
3. Sie setzte sich auf den Boden und machte eine Kerze an.

sleep	slept	slept	schlafen

Folgende Redewendungen solltest du lernen:
to sleep through something
 - etwas verschlafen, nicht mitbekommen, nicht hören (z.B. Wecker)
to sleep in
 - verschlafen; länger schlafen
to sleep on/over a question
 - ein Problem überschlafen
to sleep it off
 - seinen Rausch ausschlafen

Füge die korrekte Verbform ein.
1. He ... in the park last night.
2. ... you ever ... on a beach?
3. On Sundays we ... late.

Übersetze:
1. Hast du gerade geschlafen?
2. Wo hast du letzte Nacht geschlafen?
3. Sie sagte, sie müsse erst darüber schlafen.
4. Er sagte, er sei immer noch müde, obwohl er zehn Stunden geschlafen hatte.

smell	smelt/smelled	smelt/smelled	riechen

Folgende Redewendungen solltest du lernen:
to smell about/around
 - herumschnüffeln
to smell fishy
 - „faul" sein; nicht stimmen können

Füge die korrekte Verbform ein.
1. I told you this ... fishy, didn't I?
2. The police came to our house and ... around, asking us us a lot of questions we didn't understand.
3. The food she served us ... awful, didn't you think so?
4. She ... so badly I had to change my place.

Übersetze:
1. Ich roch, daß er Fisch gekocht hatte.
2. Sie trug ein Parfüm, das nach Seife roch.

Test 8: *Setze alle korrekten Verbformen ein (shine, shoot, show, shrink, shut, sing, sink, sit, sleep, smell):*
1. They were ... around, just doing nothing.
2. The moon ... bright and we were in a romantic mood.
3. The president ... his eyes to the people's misery.
4. I ... the sheriff but I ...n't ... the deputee.
5. He ... tight although he could see it was useless.
6. They ... a play by Tennessee Williams at the theatre last night.
7. Do you think this trousers ... ?
8. Every time I go to see him, he ... me with questions.
9. He ...n't ... up yet.
10. The flowers ... so sweet that I got a terrible headache.
11. Each time my parents said something I should not hear, they ... their voice.
12. Are you sure this shirt ...n't ... ?
13. He ... over his problem; the next day he still didn't know what to do.
14. She was so tired that she ... into sleep as soon as she lay down.

Übersetze:
1. Du mußt die Lampe auf das Bild richten (shine)!
2. Er war so verzweifelt, daß er sich erschoß (shoot).
3. Donnerstags schließen die Geschäfte erst um 20.30h (shut).
4. Billie Holiday hat in vielen Jazzclubs gesungen (sing).
5. Hast du schon mal ein Lied von Gershwin auf der Bühne gesungen (sing)?
6. Ich verstehe nicht, warum dieser Maler in Vergessenheit geraten ist (sink)!
7. Warte nicht auf mich, ich komme spät zurück (sit).
8. Er war so dick, daß alle Stühle, auf die er sich setzte, brachen (sit).
9. Ihre Kleidung riecht immer nach dem Essen, das sie gekocht hat (smell).

| speak | spoke | spoken | sprechen |

Folgende Redewendungen solltest du lernen:
not to speak of
   - ganz zu schweigen von
so to speak
   - sozusagen
to speak one's mind
   - offen seine Meinung sagen
not to be on speaking terms with someone
   - einander böse sein; nicht mehr miteinander sprechen

Füge die korrekte Verbform ein.
1. She hasn't been on ... terms with her husband for
   a couple of months.
2. She never ... of her past.
3. I ...n't yet ... to him about this matter.

Übersetze:
1. Meine Eltern sprachen nie über ihre Zukunft.
2. Sie sprach nie über ihren Freund.
3. Habt ihr schon über dein Gehalt gesprochen?
4. Trau" dich einfach, offen deine Meinung zu sagen!

| spell | spelt/spelled | spelt/spelled | buchstabieren |

Folgende Redewendung solltest du lernen:
to spell something out for someone
   - jemandem etwas genau erklären, im Detail darlegen

Füge die korrekte Verbform ein.
1. He never learned to ... my name correctly.
2. Do you think, you ... this correctly? There seems to be
   a letter missing!
3. How is your name ... ?

Übersetze:
1. Ich bat sie darum, mir ihren Plan im Detail zu erklären.
2. Meinst du, daß ich das richtig buchstabiert habe?

spend	spent	spent	verbringen, ausgeben

Folgende Redewendungen solltest du lernen:
It is money well spent.
  - Es ist sinnvoll ausgegebenes Geld; die Ausgabe hat sich
    gelohnt.
to be spent up
  - abgebrannt sein, kein Geld mehr haben

Füge die korrekte Verbform ein.

1. I ... all the money I had taken with me.
2. We ... our last holiday in Wales.
3. I ... just ... my last penny.

Übersetze:
1. Ich fürchte, wir haben all unser Geld ausgegeben.
2. Er hat sein ganzes Geld an einem einzigen Tag ausgegeben.
3. Wo habt ihr euren letzten Urlaub verbracht?

spin	span/spun	spun	spinnen, (sich) drehen

Folgende Redewendungen solltest du lernen:
to spin along
  - dahinsausen
to spin away
  - wie im Flug vergehen
to spin out a story
  - eine Geschichte in die Länge ziehen, ausdehnen, aus-
    spinnen, weiterspinnen
to spin round
  - herumwirbeln; herumfahren (sich schnell umdrehen)
my head is spinning
  - mir dreht sich alles im Kopf

Füge die korrekte Verbform ein.

1. My grandmother ... wool to earn her living.
2. When she was a child, she used to ... out the stories we
   read to her.
3. The strange noise made him ... round.

Übersetze:
1. Hast du schon mal Wolle gesponnen?
2. Ich habe zu viel Bier getrunken, und nun dreht sich mir alles im Kopf.

spread	spread	spread	(sich) ausbreiten, verbreiten

Folgende Redewendungen solltest du lernen:
to spread like wildfire
   - sich wie ein Lauffeuer verbreiten
to spread one's wings
   - versuchen, auf eigenen Beinen zu stehen; ein neues Leben anfangen
to spread oneself
   - sich viel Mühe machen als Gastgeber; sich sehr anstrengen

Füge die korrekte Verbform ein.
1. The Pacific Ocean ... before our eyes.
2. The news about the king's death ... like wildfire.
3. She ... out her arms and gave me a hug.

Übersetze:
1. Er breitete eine Decke auf der Erde aus und legte sich hin.
2. Der Vogel breitete seine Flügel aus und flog davon.
3. Die Cholera breitete sich bald über das ganze Land aus.

spring	sprang	sprung	springen

Folgende Redewendungen solltest du lernen:
to spring to the eyes
   - in die Augen springen
to spring to one's feet
   - aufspringen
to spring from
   - herkommen, herrühren von; abstammen von
to spring up
   - plötzlich entstehen, aufkommen

Füge die korrekte Verbform ein.
1. She ... up from her chair to greet me.
2. As soon as the alarm-clock rang, he ... out of bed.
3. I think I know where your misunderstanding ... from.

Übersetze:
1. Kannst du über diese Mauer springen?
2. Plötzlich sprang die Tür auf.
3. Der Fehler sprang ihm sofort in die Augen.

stand	stood	stood	stehen

Folgende Redewendungen solltest du lernen:
to stand a good chance of
   - eine gute Chance haben
his hair stands on end
   - ihm stehen die Haare zu Berge
to stand by someone
   - zu jemandem stehen; beistehen
to stand firm
   - hart bleiben; unnachgiebig sein
to stand up for someone
   - eintreten für jemanden
to stand up to someone
   - jemandem die Stirn bieten
to stand up against someone/something
   - angehen gegen jemanden/etwas
to stand someone up
   - jemanden sitzenlassen
to stand out from
   - herausragen; hervorragen
to stand together
   - zusammenhalten
to stand well with someone
   - sich mit jemandem gutstehen
to stand something on its head
   - eine Sache umdrehen, auf den Kopf stellen
to stand a test
   - eine Probe bestehen
to stand about/around
   - herumstehen

that stands out a mile
  - das sieht ja ein Blinder
and so it stands
  - und dabei bleibt es

Füge die korrekte Verbform ein.
1. ... up for your rights!
2. She ... by me when I was in trouble.
3. I'm afraid you ...n't ... the test.
4. When he saw this scene, his hair ... on end.
5. I tried to convince her but she ... firm.
6. They all ... up against their ruler.
7. I ... well with her until we had that quarrel.

Test 9: *Setze alle korrekten Verbformen ein (speak, spell, spend, spin, spread, spring, stand):*
1. As they couldn't find their key, they ... over the fence.
2. How much money ... you ... today?
3. ... you ... this out already?
4. I ... two weeks reading this book!
5. I'd really like to know where I ..., so will you please talk to me!
6. The lorry got out of its track and ... across the roadway.
7. ... this blanket over her, otherwise she will catch a cold!
8. We ... about nothing substantial last time we met.
9. He never ... to his principles.
10. I think you ... already ... too much time on this exercise.

Übersetze:
1. Habt ihr gerade über mich gesprochen (speak)?
2. Kannst du meinen Namen immer noch nicht richtig schreiben? Ich habe ihn dir doch schon mehrmals buchstabiert (spell)!
3. Wieviel Geld hast du für dein neues Fahrrad ausgegeben (spend)?
4. Die Zeit verging wie im Fluge, während er seine Geschichte erzählte (spin).
5. Die Nachricht von seiner Verlobung breitete sich wie ein Lauffeuer im Dorf aus (spread).
6. Warum bist du aufgesprungen, als ich in das Zimmer gekommen bin (spring)?
7. Sie bot ihrem Vater die Stirn (stand).

steal	stole	stolen	stehlen

Folgende Redewendungen solltest du lernen:
to steal away
   - sich davonstehlen
to steal a glance at someone
   - einen verstohlenen Blick werfen auf

Füge die korrekte Verbform ein.
1. He ... the money and run away.
2. I can't find my bike. Someone must ... it.
3. He ... a glance at her hands.
4. She ... his thunder by reminding him of his own faults.

Übersetze:
1. Ich mag meinen Bruder nicht; er stiehlt mir immer die Show.
2. Ich weiß nicht, wo er sein neues Auto her hat. Wahrscheinlich hat er es gestohlen.
3. Warum hast du diese Halskette gestohlen? Sie ist nichts wert!

stick	stuck	stuck	stecken, kleben

Folgende Redewendungen solltest du lernen:
to stick by someone
   - zu jemandem halten; treu bleiben
to be stuck on someone
   - in jemanden vernarrt sein
to stick in one's mind
   - in jemandes Gedächtnis haften bleiben
to stick to the point
   - bei der Sache bleiben

Füge die korrekte Verbform ein.
1. I am glad you ... by me when I needed you.
2. Don't you see he's completely ... on her?
3. His words ... in her mind.

Übersetze:
1. Hast du die Briefmarke schon auf den Brief geklebt?

2. Leider hat sie nicht zu mir gehalten.
3. Das hat nichts damit zu tun. Bitte bleib bei der Sache!

sting	stung	stung	stechen

Folgende Redewendung solltest du lernen:
to be stung with remorse
- von Reue geplagt sein

Füge die korrekte Verbform ein.
1. A bee ... me in the foot.
2. The smoke of her cigarette ... my eyes.
3. Take care, these nettles ... !

Übersetze:
1. Ihre bissige Bemerkung hat mich sehr verletzt.
2. Ich habe mir mit einer Nadel in den Finger gestochen.
3. Bist du dir sicher, daß dich der Skorpion gestochen hat?

strike	struck	struck	schlagen

Folgende Redewendungen solltest du lernen:
to strike a blow against someone
- jemandem einen Schlag versetzen
to strike for/against something
- streiken für/gegen etwas
to strike a match
- ein Streichholz anzünden
to strike someone's eye
- jemandem ins Auge fallen
to strike at the root of something
- etwas an der Wurzel treffen
to strike the right note
- den richtigen Ton treffen

Füge die korrekte Verbform ein.
1. She ... a match to light her cigarette.
2. He really ... my eye.
3. I think he ... a false note when he complained about me.
4. I told you she would ... it rich one day (das große Los ziehen)!

Übersetze:
1. Ich bin froh, daß er den richtigen Ton getroffen hat.
2. Mir ist dieses Bild gleich ins Auge gefallen.
3. Sie streikten für höhere Löhne.

strive	strove	striven	streben

Folgende Redewendung solltest du lernen:
to strive after effects
   - Effekte haschen wollen

Füge die korrekte Verbform ein.
1. He never ... for happiness.
2. I ... always ... towards good relationships.

Übersetze:
1. In ihrer Jugend strebte sie danach, Ballettänzerin zu werden.
2. Glaubst du nicht, daß sie nach Glück strebte?
3. Damals strebte ich noch nach Ruhm, aber so dumm bin ich nicht mehr.

swear	swore	sworn	schwören

Folgende Redewendungen solltest du lernen:
to swear by all one holds dear
   - schwören bei allem, was einem heilig ist
to swear by something
   - schwören auf etwas; fest glauben an etwas; von etwas überzeugt sein
to swear someone in
   - jemanden vereidigen
to swear off something
   - einer Sache (Laster) abschwören

Füge die korrekte Verbform ein.
1. When will you be ... in?
2. She finally ... off drinking.
3. He ... by the life of his grandmother that he hadn't been responsible for the hold-up.

1. Ich hätte schwören können, daß ich sie zusammen gesehen habe.
2. Sie schwor immer, die Wahrheit zu sagen und log dann doch.
3. Er schwor bei allem, was ihm heilig war, so daß ich ihm schließlich glaubte.

sweat	sweat/sweated	sweat/sweated	schwitzen

Folgende Redewendungen solltest du lernen:
to sweat blood over something
- Blut und Wasser schwitzen; sich abrackern für etwas

Füge die korrekte Verbform ein.
1. We ... a lot during our holiday in India.
2. He ... a great deal during his way up the hill.
3. I ... so much that I have to take a shower right now.

Übersetze:
1. Ich habe mich für diese Prüfung abgerackert und sie doch nicht bestanden.
2. Ich war überrascht; ich hätte nie gedacht, daß sie durchhält (to sweat it out).

sweep	swept	swept	fegen, kehren

Folgende Redewendungen solltest du lernen:
to sweep across one's mind
- einem in den Sinn kommen
to sweep something aside
- beiseite schieben; ignorieren (z.B. Argumente, Ratschläge, Einwände)
to sweep someone off his feet
- jemanden mitreißen, „umhauen', überwältigen
to sweep something away
- etwas mitreißen, umreißen, fortreißen
to sweep away someone's doubts
- jemandes Zweifel ausräumen

Füge die korrekte Verbform ein.
1. She ... out of the room like a fury.
2. ... you ... your room yet?
3. He ... away my doubts with a smile.

Übersetze:
1. Du hättest wenigstens den Boden kehren können!
2. Die Flut hat mehrere Häuser mitgerissen.
3. Du hättest seine Zweifel so leicht ausräumen können!

swim	swam	swum	schwimmen

Folgende Redewendungen solltest du lernen:
to swim in money
   - im Geld schwimmen
to swim before one's eyes
   - vor den Augen verschwimmen

Füge die korrekte Verbform ein.
1. Her eyes ... with tears.
2. Last year, they ... in money.
3. The letters ... before his eyes.

Übersetze:
1. Sie schwamm ans Ufer und brach vollkommen erschöpft zusammen.
2. Er schwamm schneller als ich und kam als erster an.
3. Wir schwammen auf die kleine Insel und blieben den ganzen Tag dort.

swing	swung	swung	schwingen

Folgende Redewendungen solltest du lernen:
to swing into action
   - loslegen
to swing the lead
   - sich vor der Arbeit drücken; krankfeiern
to swing something
   - etwas schon hinkriegen; das Kind schon schaukeln
to swing round

- sich ruckartig umdrehen
no room to swing a cat in
- sehr eng; kein Bewegungsraum

Füge die korrekte Verbform ein.
1. O.K., now let's ... into action!
2. The actor ... round and started reciting his text.
3. She ... her arms to keep her balance.

Übersetze:
1. Sie drehte sich ruckartig um, als ich das Zimmer betrat.
2. Er ritt auf einem Pferd durch die Pampa und schwang sein Lasso.
3. Er hat sich gestern vor der Arbeit gedrückt.

take	took	taken	bringen, nehmen

Folgende Redewendungen solltest du lernen:
to take something amiss
- etwas übelnehmen
to take something at face value
- etwas für bare Münze nehmen
to take something for granted
- etwas als selbstverständlich ansehen, hinnehmen
to take a look at something
- sich etwas anschauen
to take to one's heels
- sich aus dem Staub machen; die Beine in die Hand nehmen
to take notes
- sich Notizen machen; mitschreiben
to take notice of something
- etwas beachten
to take place
- stattfinden
to take one's leave
- sich verabschieden
to take one's time
- sich Zeit lassen
to take someone at his word
- jemanden beim Wort nehmen

to take someone for someone else
- jemanden mit jemandem verwechseln
to take someone for a ride
- jemanden auf eine Spazierfahrt mitnehmen
to be taken for a ride
- auf die Schippe genommen werden
to take turns with someone
- sich mit jemandem abwechseln
Take it easy!
- Nimm's leicht!
Take it or leave it!
- Mach, was du willst!

Füge die korrekte Verbform ein.
1. They ... us for a ride last Sunday.
2. They could ... their leave earlier, don't you think so, too?
3. He ... all the money with him when he left me.
4. You shouldn't ... this seriously!
5. He ... your remark to heart.
6. He ... her in his arms and gave her a hug.
7. It ... me quite a lot of time to get my bike repaired.

Übersetze:
1. Wieviel Fahrstunden hast du bis jetzt genommen?
2. Sie beachtete ihn einfach nicht.
3. Laß" dir ruhig Zeit!
4. Hast du die Briefe schon zur Post gebracht?

Test 10: *Setze alle korrekten Verbformen ein (steal, stick, sting, strike, strive, swear, sweat, sweep, swim, take):*
1. She ... away at night.
2. He ... into the room without being seen.
3. Her idea ... me as quite interesting.
4. He ... at the problem until he had solved it.
5. What really ... me was that she didn't tell me anything about it.
6. She ... for fame and fortune.
7. She ... not to tell anybody.
8. I'm afraid, he ... me for your mother!
9. Yesterday's spectacle just ... me off my feet.
10. The master made his servant ... .
11. She ... blood over this matter.

12. His behaviour ... me as really odd.
13. ... you already ... a look at the book I gave you?
14. We were ... and had to pass the night in the wood.
15. She ... the whole affair under the carpet.
16. She ... never ... against the tide.
17. We ... across the river.
18. He sat on a bench ... his legs.
19. The door ... open and in she came!
20. He ... her hand and kissed it.

Übersetze:
1. Die Diebe haben alles gestohlen, was wir hatten (steal).
2. Seine ständigen Beleidigungen taten ihr sehr weh (sting).
3. Er strebte nie nach Perfektion (strive).
4. Plötzlich kam ihr etwas in den Sinn (sweep).

teach	taught	taught	lehren, unterrichten

Folgende Redewendungen solltest du lernen:
to teach someone a lesson
   - jemandem eine Lektion erteilen
That'll teach you!
   - Das wird dir eine Lehre sein!

Füge die korrekte Verbform ein.
1. My mother ... me how to write.
2. ... you ... your dog this new trick?
3. How did you manage to ... your cat standing on its nose?

Übersetze:
1. Ihre Eltern haben ihr nicht beigebracht, wie man sich gut benimmt.
2. Ihr habt mir das neue Spiel noch nicht beigebracht.
3. Du hättest deinem Hund beibringen können, die Tür zu öffnen.

Achtung: You can't teach an old dog new tricks.
Was Hänschen nicht lernt, lernt Hans nimmermehr.

tear	tore	torn	(zer)reißen

Folgende Redewendungen solltest du lernen:
to tear to pieces
   - in Stücke reißen
to tear one's hair
   - sich die Haare raufen
to tear something to shreds
   - etwas völlig „zerreißen", total niedermachen, vernichtend
    kritisieren (z.B. Buch)

Füge die korrekte Verbform ein.

1. She ... his farewell letter to pieces.
2. We ...n't ... off the wallpaper yet.

Übersetze:
1. Ich hätte mir die Haare raufen können!
2. Er riß die Rechnung in Stücke und verließ das
    Restaurant.
3. Diesen Karton zerreißt du nicht so leicht.

tell	told	told	sagen, erzählen

Folgende Redewendungen solltest du lernen:
to tell tales
   - flunkern
it is hard to tell
   - es ist schwer zu sagen
you can never tell
   - man kann nie wissen

Füge die korrekte Verbform ein.

1. I don't believe a word he says; he ... already ... me so
    many lies!
2. He ... it to my face without the slightest regard to
    decency.
3. She ... us a most irritating story about a murder in the
    neighbourhood.

Übersetze:
1. Ich weiß, daß die Lage hoffnungslos aussieht, aber man
    kann nie wissen!

think	thought	thought	denken

Folgende Redewendungen solltest du lernen:
to think something over
   - sich etwas überlegen
I thought as much
   - das habe ich mir gedacht
to think something up
   - etwas ersinnen, aushecken

Füge die korrekte Verbform ein.
1. I ... you had already left!
2. ... you ever ... about leaving him?
3. I guess he always ... I loved him.

Übersetze:
1. Wer hätte das gedacht!
2. Er dachte, es würde regnen.
3. Ich hätte nie gedacht, daß wir uns wiedersehen würden!
4. Wir dachten, ihr wäret schon abgereist.

throw	threw	thrown	werfen

Folgende Redewendungen solltest du lernen:
to throw oneself into something
   - sich intensiv mit einer Sache beschäftigen
to throw light on something
   - Licht auf eine Sache werfen
to throw someone off
   - jemanden abschütteln, loswerden
to throw one's weight about
   - sich aufspielen
to throw doubt on something
   - Zweifel an etwas aufkommen lassen

Füge die korrekte Verbform ein.
1. I can't believe that he was ... off the horse's back!
2. Why ... you ... the newspaper away?
3. The children ... stones at the birds.
4. They ... the ball to me but I didn't catch it.

Übersetze:
1. Hat dich dieses Pferd jemals abgeworfen?
2. Sobald er auf der Straße war, übergab er sich.
3. Seine Zeugenaussage wirft neues Licht auf den Mordfall.

understand	understood	understood	verstehen

Folgende Redewendungen solltest du lernen:
I understand that ...
    - Ich nehme an, daß; ich höre, daß
What do you understand by this?
    - Was verstehen Sie darunter?

Füge die korrekte Verbform ein.
1. ... you ... the meaning of this phrase?
2. I don't think he ... what I was telling him.
3. My grandmother never ... me.

Übersetze:
1. Ich nehme an, daß Sie Lehrer sind.
2. Du hast mich bestimmt verstanden, nicht wahr?
3. Warum versteht sie mich nie?

wear	wore	worn	tragen, anhaben

Folgende Redewendungen solltest du lernen:
to wear on someone's nerves
    - jemandem auf die Nerven gehen
to wear out
    - sich abnutzen, abtragen (z.B. Kleidung)
to wear someone out
    - jemanden ermüden; jemandes Geduld erschöpfen
to wear out one's welcome
- länger bleiben als man erwünscht ist

Füge die korrekte Verbform ein.
1. What ... you ... at your brother's wedding?
2. She always ... red clothes.
3. This jeans is really ... out.
4. I think she ... a blue dress.
5. This time he really ... out his welcome.

Übersetze:
1. Ich glaube, er trug einen grauen Hut.
2. Hast du schon mal einen Bart getragen?
3. Warum trägst du nie Jeans?

Hinweis: wear and tear - Verschleiß

weep	wept	wept	weinen

Folgende Redewendung solltest du lernen:
to have a good weep
 - sich tüchtig ausweinen

Füge die korrekte Verbform ein.
1. She ... all night long.
2. Why ... you ... ?
3. The bad news made him ... .

Übersetze:
1. Du hättest dir wegen ihr nicht die Augen ausweinen sollen
2. Sie weinte sich jede Nacht in den Schlaf.
3. Warum hast du geweint, als du sie gesehen hast?
4. Er weinte eine ganze Woche lang über sein Schicksal.

win	won	won	gewinnen

Folgende Redewendungen solltest du lernen.
to win fame
 - sich Ruhm erwerben
to win hands down
 - ohne Anstrengung gewinnen; leicht gewinnen
to win someone's heart/love
 - jemandes Herz/Liebe gewinnen
to win one's bread
 - sein Brot verdienen
to win someone over to something
 - jemanden für etwas gewinnen

Füge die korrekte Verbform ein.
1. She ... his heart at once.
2. She finally ... fame.
3. O.K., you ... this time.

Übersetze:
1. Wer hat das letzte Spiel gewonnen?
2. Ich habe mein ganzes Geld auf das schwarze Pferd gesetzt, aber leider hat es das Rennen nicht gewonnen.
3. Du hättest den Preis leicht gewinnen können.

| write | wrote | written | schreiben |

Folgende Redewendung solltest du lernen:
written in water
   - in den Wind geschrieben; vergänglich

Füge die korrekte Verbform ein.
1. Who ... you this letter?
2. Hemingway ... quite a lot of books.
3. ... you ever ... a novel?

Übersetze:
1. Warum hast du mir in all den Jahren nie geschrieben?
2. Tennessee Williams hat Theaterstücke geschrieben.
3. Wer hat die Bibel geschrieben?
4. Er schrieb immer auf rotem Papier.
5. Ich kenne diese Handschrift nicht; hast du das
   geschrieben?

Abschlußtest

BEGIN: 1. You can still join us, we ...n't ... yet. BEND: 2. Don't ... over the table while eating. Sit upright! BITE: 3. She said she wanted to taste the hamburger I was eating and ... off half of it. 4. Although it looks quite mean, this dog ... never ... anyone. BREAK: 5. He became furious when he learned that we ... the tea-pot his mother had given him. BURST: 6. She told me that this man ... already ... out of prison twice. 7. He was ... to give us his present. BUY: 8. He was ... over by a terrorist organization. 9. He ... a new suit for his friend's wedding. CATCH: 10. The title of this book immediately ... my eye. CHOOSE: 11. Your job seems to be interesting. I think you ... well. CLING: 12. They ... always ... together. DEAL: 13. He wrote a book that ... with biology. DIG: 14. We ... up all the ground in search for water but we haven't found any so far. DRAW: 15. She ... a gun and threatened to shoot him. DRINK: 16. The students ... in their professor's words. FEEL: 17. I ... always ... that this thing wasn't going to last. 18. He ... like crying. FIGHT: 19. He ... back his tears so that people wouldn't notice his distress. 20. We ... over this silly matter a lot of times. FIND: 21. I ... just ... out that my husband started betraying me even before we got married. 22. I ...n't ... the record you asked me for yet but I will keep on looking for it. FORGET: 23. I'm afraid he is getting old. He ... everything you tell him. FORGIVE: 24. Please, tell me: am I ... ? FREEZE: 25. I felt ... so I took a bath. GET: 26. He ... me wrong and now he's angry with me. GIVE: 27. She ... birth to a boy. GO: 28. When I finally arrived at the meetingplace, they ... already ... HAVE: 29. Last summer I ... the time of my life! HEAR: 30. I never ... a more silly story in all my life! HIDE: 31. The treasure was ... in our garden. KNOW: 32. She never ... how to treat children. LEAP: 33. The horse ... over the fence and broke its leg. LEND: 34. I ... him my bike and I'm not sure if I shall ever see it again. LIE: 35. Mr Jones ... in hospital for two months. READ: 36. I had him ... the letter out. RIDE: 37. Cowboys don't ... on horses anymore. RUN: 38. Whe ... out of burning wood. Would you go out to get some? SEE: 39. Yesterday I ... a play at the theatre. 40. We ...n't ... much of you lately! SEEK: 41. You shouldn't ... to convince her! SELL: 42. ... you ... any of these jeans yet? SEND: 43. His fever rose so high that we had ... for a doctor in the middle of the night. SET: 44. I'm afraid I forgot ... the alarm-clock. 45. Scott ... out for an expedition in 1912 and never came back. SHAKE: 46. His voice ... with emotion when he asked her to marry him. 47. She ... her head in surprise. SHOOT: 48. The police caught him as he ... the lights. 49. The motorbike ... past us, covering us with dust. SHUT: 50. She put the letter into the drawer and ... it. SING: 51. By whom is this song you just ... ? SINK: 52. When he saw his rival, his heart ... into his boots. SIT: 53. We ... in the last row so we didn't see much of the spectacle. SPEAK: 54. When I finally ... my mind, the effect of it was that he got very angry at me. SPREAD: 55. ... you already ... the table? 56. Why ...n't you ... any jam on your toast? SPRING: 57. When I got that call, a suspicion ... up in my mind. TEACH: 58. I'm trying to forget the nonsense he ... me. 59. Would you like me ... you playing the piano? 60. We weren't ... Spanish at school. TEAR: 61. The critic ... the new play to shreds. 62. Why ... you ... off your clothes? You will catch cold! 63. Our house ... down after we moved out. TELL: 64. ...n't I ... you a hundred times to be careful with this   knife? 65. He ... me about all his problems. It took us about a week or so. THINK: 66. I ... a lot about this problem but I haven't found a solution yet. 67. I guess she ... something up. 68. I ... never ... about breaking up this relationship. THROW: 69. He was ... into prison injustly. UNDERSTAND: 70. I think, you ...n't ... me right. 71. I'm really not sure he ... . WEAR: 72. You should really ... your glasses. WEEP: 73. When they saw me again, they ... for joy. WIN: 74. They ... him over to their opinion. 75. She ... the tennis match hands down. 76. The enemy's troops ... the battle. 77. ... you ever ... a prize before? WRITE: 78. She ... down her address and gave it to me. 79. Their love was ... in water. 80. Aunt Laurie ...n't ... me a Christmas card this year.

Lösungen:

AWAKE: 1. awaken 2. will awaken 3. awoke 1. Suddenly a strange noise awoke me. 2. On Sundays the children never awoke before 9 o'clock. 3. When he awoke, it had stopped raining. BE: 1. was 2. has been 3. were 4. were 1. He has been in London for ten days. 2. The exam was quite difficult for the pupils. 3. They have already been to four museums. BEAR: 1. bear 2. bore* 3. was born 4. have born 1. I can't bear this noise. 2. She was born in Amsterdam. 3. He bore his father's name. 4. When were you born? BEAT: 1. beaten 2. beat 3. beating 4. was beaten* 1. She always beat me at chess. 2. He beat on the door several times. 3. He was beating the drum. BECOME: 1. became 2. had become 3. have become 4. became 1. It became warmer. 2. At last he became accustomed to the weather in India. 3. Jeans have become quite expensive. BEGIN: 1. began* 2. has begun 3. began 4. began 5. have begun* 1. When we switched on the TV, the film had already begun. 2. She began getting nervous. 3. Rehearsals will begin in March. BEND: 1. bent 2. bent 1. He bent down to pick up a coin. 2. She had bent forward and was listening to us attentively. BIND: 1. bound 2. bound 1. We were bound to discretion. 2. The burglar had bound the landlord to the chair. BITE: 1. have been bitten 2. bit* 1. The angler got angry because the fish would't bite. 2. The postman was bitten by a hostile dog. 3. I bit mmy tongue. BLEED: 1. bleeding 2. bleeding* 1. The wound was bleeding so badly he lost his consciousness. 2. If we don't call a doctor immediately, he will bleed to death. BLOW: 1. blew 2. blew 3. blowing 1. The wind blew out the candle. 2. The wind has blown the hat off his head. BREAK: 1. broke 2. broken 1. She broke a valuable vase. 2. His funny remark broke the ice. BRING: 1. brought* 2. brought* 3. has brought* 4. was brought* 1. Their conversation brought him down to earth. 2. I can't leave because she hasn't yet brought back the car. 3. Come and bring your friends along with you! BUILD: 1. built 2. built* 3. build 4. built 1. This house was built in only two months. 2. Do you know how the pyramids were built? 3. Their relationship was built on sand; it was bound to fail. 4. The new school is to be built next year.

Test 1: 1. were* 2. have become 3. bore* 4. beat 5. awaken 6. bitten 7. built 8. began 9. had bound* 10. broke* 11. bend 12. bleed 13. bled 14. blow 15. bring

ÜBERSETZUNG: 1. As soon as she awoke, she got up. 2. We were really shocked when we heard about the accident. 3. Yesterday I got a letter that bore no signature. 4. The rain kept beating against the window all night long. 5. He has become a tourist guide. 6. Only a few English words begin with a 'K'. 7. He always bent the pages of his books. 8. The doctor bound the wound. 9. Have you ever been bitten by a cat? 10. He blew the dust off the book, opened it on the first page and began to read. 11. She broke her leg when she slipped in the tub. 12. He always brought along his girlfriend when I invited him for dinner. 13. The sea has washed away the sand-castle we built yesterday.

BURST: 1. burst 2. burst 1. When she learned about the accident, she burst into tears. 1. He burst into the room without knocking on the door. BUY: 1. bought 2. have bought* 1. I haven't yet bought the books you asked me for. 2. They will buy a house at the seaside. 3. I haven't bought the tickets yet. CAST: 1. to cast 2. cast 1. They cast the blame for the failure of the plan on me. 2. Her essay cast a new light on the problem of whaling. CATCH: 1. caught 2. caught 1. He caught the ball and threw it back to me. 2. They haven't caught the thief yet. CHOOSE: 1. choose 2. chose* 1. The suit you chose is very becoming. 2. Have you already chosen? CLING: 1. clung 2. clung 1. His clothes clung to his body for he had been walking through the rain. COME: 1. came* 2. hasn't come 3. hasn't come 4. came 1. He didn't come to our party last night. 2. When the conflict came to a head, they finally entered into negotiations. 3. He has come to get his suitcases. 4. When I was in hospital she came to see me every day. 5. I came across this photograph looking through your letters. COST: cost 2. cost 3. cost* 1. The race cost him his life. 2. Last year, coals cost less. CREEP: 1. crept 2. creep 3. creeping 1. He crept silently into the room. 2. Your playing the violin makes my flesh creep. CUT: 1. cut 2. cut 3. cut 4. cut* 5. have cut. 1. I was in such a hurry that I cut my face while shaving. 2. I cut out all newspaper articles that interest me. 3. Cardboard doesn't cut easily. 4. I had my hair cut yesterday. 5. Since we have cut the grass, we can sit in the garden again.

Test 2: 1. came 2. cast* 3. haven't chosen 4. have caught* 5. have cut 6. cost 7. to catch 8. have caught 9. had clung 10. crept* 11. to cast

ÜBERSETZUNG: 1. If the tyre hadn't burst, the accident wouldn't have happened. 2. He hasn't bought himself a car yet. 3. When we accused her of having stolen the money, she cast her eyes down and went out of the room. 4. They caught him when he tried to set the house on fire. 5. He caught his breath and stole into the room. 6. The restaurant he had chosen was both cheap and bad. 7. I don't like this hat. My mother chose it for me. 8. They couldn't choose but accept his decision. 9. As I couldn't see anything, I clung to her arm. 10. She came back to apologize. 11. Last year coals cost less. 12. He crept under the table looking for a coin he had lost. 13. He cut an enormous slice of cake.

DEAL: 1. dealt 2. dealt 1. Last time it was you who dealt the cards, this time it is my turn. DIG: 1. have dug* 2. haven't dug 1. You haven't dug deep enough yet. 2. For years they dug for gold but they never found any. DIVE: 1. dived/dove 2. dived/dove* 1. He dived/dove into the sea and stayed under the water for four minutes. DO: 1. did* 2. haven't done 3. did 4. do 5. did 6. have been doing 7. did 8. have done 9. did 1. He did his best to save her. 2. He did it on purpose. 3. I haven't done the dishes yet. 4. Did you do your homework? 5. What did you do in August? 6. You shouldn't have done that! DRAW: 1. drew 2. drew 3. has drawn 1. I cannot draw a conclusion from her statement. 2. She drew a breath and dived into the water. DRINK: 1. has drunk 2. haven't drunk 1. He could have drunk me under the table if he had wanted to. 2. He drank his troubles away. 3. She has died for having drunk too much. DRIVE: 1. Has been driving 2. drove 3. has driven 1. He drove very carefully. 2. I have been driving this car for eight years. 3. They called the police and drove on. EAT: 1. haven't eaten 2. ate 3. have eaten 4. ate 1. He never invited her to a restaurant because she ate like a horse. 2. She's behaving strangely. Do you know, what's eating her? 3. We started eating in when we ran out of money. FALL: 1. fell 2. fell 3. fall 1. In the desert, the temperature falls considerably at night. 2. When the boxer saw his opponent, his courage fell. 3. The teapot fell from the table and broke into pieces. 4. I have fallen down and broken my leg. FEED: 1. could feed 2. haven't fed 3. fed 1. What do you feed your cat on? 2. She preferred feeding her baby at the breast. 3. He doesn't feed the cat regularly. FEEL: 1. felt 2. felt 1. I have never felt so blue as today. 2. I feel like going for a walk. Do you want to come with me? FIGHT: 1. to fight 2. fought* 1. They have been fighting for their independence for many years. 2. She fought tooth and nail to obtain an exit visa. FIND: 1. found 2. have found 1. They dug their garden until they found the treasure. FLEE: 1. fled 2. fled 1. The enemies fled when our army appeared at the horizon. 2. I haven't the slightest respect for her because she flees every danger. FLY: 1. flies 2. have flown 3. flew 4. flew* 1. We flew over the Atlantic Ocean. 2. She flew into my arms as soon as she saw me. 3. Look, what time it is! We must fly! 4. The door flew open and in came Tom.

Test 3: 1. dived/dove 2. dug 3. flies 4. have fallen* 5. has been drinking 6. have been dealing* 7. haven't eaten 8. have fed* 9. are driving 10. found* 11. felt 12. flew 13. fought 14. have flown* 15. drew

ÜBERSETZUNG: 1. So far we have dealt in hats but now we deal in canes, too. 2. Have you ever dived in the Pacific Ocean? 3. I should have drawn this scene! 4. She has been drinking since her early youth. 5. It was very late when we drove home from the party. 6. They used to eat out a lot. 7. I was frightened so much that I let the burning candle fall down. 8. He went home because he was feeling ill. 9. She felt so sad she couldn't fight back her tears. 10. I fled from the police. 11. The bird broke its wing and now it can't fly any more. 12. I have never flown on this airline before.

FORBID: 1. forbade* 2. forbidden 3. forbade* 1. God forbid that he comes back! 2. He forbade us to leave the house while the storm lasted. 3. It is forbidden to touch the goods in this store. FORGET: 1. forgot* 2. have forgotten 3. forget 4. forgot* 5. have forgotten 6. have forgotten* 1. She always forgot something at my house. 2. I have forgotten all of my French. 3. I forgot my suitcase on the train. FORGIVE: 1. forgave 2. forgive 3. forgave* 4. forgive 1. When we weren't able to pay, she forgave us our debt. 2. He said, he would never forgive me. 3. She was glad we forgave her. FREEZE: 1. froze 2. froze 3. froze 1. The lake was frozen. 2. The ghost's appearance made her blood freeze. 3. The didn't find the way back and froze to death. 4. Just freeze the food that was left over! GET: 1. got 2. got 3. get 4. got 1. What have you got there? 2. Look, what I have got from my parents! 3. You will have to get along with her, like it or not! 4. You look so angry. What has got into you? 5. O.k., let's get over with this discussion. 6. He was still here at midnight. I just couldn't get rid of him. GIVE: 1. gave 2. gave 3. haven't given 4. give 1. You just gave up too soon. You should have tried a little harder. 2. I will give you the book as soon as I have read it. 3. She gave a smile to me and dissappeared. 4. Don't forget, you gave me your word not to tell anybody. 5. How much money have I given you until now? GO: 1. went* 2. have gone 3. have gone* 4. went 5. go 6. gone 7. went 8. have gone 9. has gone* 10. went 11. went* 1. He went on and on about his operation. 2. Our king used to say that you had to go with the times. 3. Do you know which of these roads goes to Bath? 4. I went in there by pure chance.

Test 4: 1. got 2. forget 3. forbade* 4. forbidden 5. have forbidden* 6. forbade 7. forgotten 8. have given* 9. has forgiven 10. forgiven 11. have forgiven 12. forgiven 13. forgive 14. frozen 15. forgot* 16. has forgotten* 17. freezing 18. get 19. has forgiven* 20. have given

ÜBERSETZUNG: 1. The waiter is furious because one guest has forgotten to pay his meal. 2. I forgot to make a reservation at the restaurant. 3. Please, forgive me for having been not too friendly to you. 4. Have you forgiven me? 5. You should never have forgiven her! 6. They couldn't dig up the ground because it was frozen. 7. I haven't got your letter yet. 8. This band has never given a concert before. 9. I have to call her. Do you know where she has gone to?

GROW: 1. had grown 2. to grow 3. had grown 1. You haven't grown at all since the last time I saw you. 2. Look, how my hair has grown! 3. The floor has grown much darker since we removed the carpet. HANG: 1. hung 2. have hung 3. hangs 1. Have you already hung the washing? 2. Not a single picture hung on his wall. HAVE: 1. haven't had 2. had 3. has 4. had 5. didn't have 6. had 7. has 1. I haven't had any news from her since she left. 2. He has an extremely bad memory. 3. You may have this jacket if you feel cold. 4. I had a strange dream last night. 5. We had one of those endless discussions that lead to nothing. HEAR: 1. have heard* 2. didn't hear 1. There was a noise. I heard it distinctly! 2. She never heard me out. HIDE: 1. hid 2. hid 1. He never managed to hide his feelings. 2. It seems to me that you have something to hide, am I right? HIT: 1. hit 2. hit 1. He hit the nail on the head with his remark. HOLD: 1. hold 2. hold 3. held* 1. She seems nervous. I'm sure she's holding something back from us. 2. I hold the view that lions shouldn't be hunted. HURT: 1. hurt 2. hurt 3. hurt 4. haven't hurt 1. I hope you didn't hurt yourself. 2. These shoes hurt me from the beginning. 3. You hurt his feelings with your silly behaviour. KEEP: 1. keep 2. kept 3. kept* 4. keep 5. have kept 6. kept 7. kept* 1. They came together to the dinner party to keep up appearances. 2. Please, try to keep in mind our appointment on Monday. 3. I was amazed at how cool he kept. 4. He has kept fit by jogging every day. 5. I hope you don't mind that I kept the book so long. KNOW: 1. knew 2. have known 3. knew 1. I knew that our plan would fail. 2. She knew she would see him again. LAY: 1. laid* 2. laid 1. Danny laid the table. 2. I don't know where I laid my hat. 3. Hens lay eggs. 4. Where did she lay the newspaper? LEAD: 1. led* 2. led 1. I was sure this was going to lead up to a quarrel. 2. The road we took led to Edinburgh. LEAP: 1. leapt/leaped* 2. leapt/leaped* 1. The dog hurt me when it leapt/leaped up at me. 2. She leapt/leaped into the lake without having a reason to do so. LEAVE: 1. left 2. left 1. They left for France last night. 2. She has left me for a younger man. 3. I thought you had left your husband since long. LEND: 1. lent* 2. lent* 1. How much money did you lend him? 2. Is this your car? – No, David lent it to me. LET: 1. let 2. let 3. let. 1. Let's go for a swim! 2. She let me know that she wouldn't come. 3. My boyfriend always let me wear his hats. LIE: 1. lay* 2. lie 3. lay* 1. The old castle lay in ruins. 2. The snow lay thick on the branches of the trees.

Test 5: 1. have grown 2. haven't heard 3. hang 4. has 5. grew* 6. heard 7. has hidden 8. had hidden 9. was hit 10. was holding* 11. hurt 12. hurt 13. leaped/leapt 14. let 15. held 16. left 17. led 18. has held 19. lying 20. hit* 21. left 22. lent 23. knew 24. knew 25. to have 26. kept 27. left* 28. have left* 29. led* 30. have lent* 31. lies 32. left

LIGHT: 1. lit 2. lit 1. The room was lit by candles exclusively. 2. His eyes lit up when I told him that she had come back. LOOSE: 1. has lost 2. have lost* 1. We lost all our money on horse-racing. 2. I'm glad to see you haven't lost your self-confidence. 3. I'm afraid to tell my landlord that I have lost the keys. MAKE: 1. had made 2. made* 3. have made 4. made* 5. made 6. has made 1. I made a cake for tonight's party. 2. Just wait a minute, I haven't made coffee yet. 3. She made herself a cup of tea and sat on the sofa. 4. He made himself comfortable on the sofa. 5. When she realized how late it was, she lept up and made for the door. 6. He tried to make believe that he wasn't interested at all. 7. He has made no good impression on me. 8. I made a silly mistake. 9. The clown made us laugh. MEAN: 1. meant 2. meant 1. I'm sorry, I didn't mean to disturb you. 2. Are you sure that her remark was meant to be a joke? MEET: 1. met 2. met 1. Unfortunately, my suggestion met with a refusal. 2. We met in New York by chance. PAY: 1. haven't paid 2. paid 1. He never paid her compliments. 2. Last year, we finally paid off our house. 3. He never paid his debts. PUT: 1. put 2. have put* 3. have put* 4. put* 5. have put* 6. put 1. Are you looking for the keys? I have put them on the table. 2. She put her feet on the table and switched on the TV. 3. Have you put on your raincoat? 4. I put the food that was left over in the refrigerator.

Test 6: 1. paid 2. lit 3. lost 4. meant 5. lit 6. made 7. meant 8. have put* 9. lost 10. met 11. to meet 12. met 13. will pay 14. met* 15. paid 16. lit 17. paid* 18. has lost* 19. put

ÜBERSETZUNG: 1. The fire in the fire place lit the whole room. 2. Do you know whether he lost his leg in the war? 3. Your love meant a great deal to me. 4. Is this present meant for your grandmother? 5. I have just met my wife with another man. 6. I prefer paying cash. 7. Have you already paid your bills? 8. Where have you put the money I gave you?

READ: 1. have read* 2. read 1. Have you already read the new novel by Stephen King? 2. Have you ever read a novel by Hemingway? RIDE: 1. have ridden 2. ridden 1. Have you ever ridden on an elephant? 2. The bandit shot his rival and rode away on a white horse. RING: 1. rings* 2. rang 3. haven't rung 1. Doesn't this ring a bell? 2. I think someone has rung the doorbell. RISE: 1. rise 2. has risen 1. The curtain rose and the actors appeared on the stage. 2. The prices for fur coats have risen remarkably during the last ten years. RUN: 1. ran 2. has run 1. I ran as fast as I could. 2. She has run away from home. 3. He ran across the street to catch his dog. SAY: 1. said 2. said* 3. said 1. He said it hadn't been easy to get an invitation. 2. I didn't understand a single word of what he said. 3. It is hard to say who will win. 4. She seems angry. What did you say to her? SEE: 1. did see 2. saw 3. haven't seen 4. saw* 5. saw 6. had seen 1. I saw him only once. 2. Have you already seen the new movie by Saura? 3. It was very nice of you to see me home. 4. Have you ever seen a bear? 5. It was so foggy that we couldn't see anything. SEEK: 1. sought 2. sought* 1. These typewriters are much sought after. 2. At last we sought out uncle Toby in Hongkong. SELL: 1. sold 2. have been sold 1. They sold their house and got a divorce. 2. The play was sold out in an hour. SEND: 1. hasn't sent 2. sent 1. The parents sent their children to bed and went to the cinema. 2. Have you ever sent a telegram to your grandparents? SET: 1. set 2. have set 3. set 4. is set. 5. set 6. have set. 1. Have you already set up your new refrigerator? 2. The prisoner was set free only last week. 3. They will set out on their journey round the world next week. 4. She has set her mind on going off to Alaska. 5. I am dead set against your silly plan. 6. The sun hasn't set yet. SHAKE: 1. to shake 2. shook 3. shake 4. shook 1. Why did you shake your head? 2. I didn't manage to shake off my pursuer. 3. She never shook hands with me. SHED: 1. didn't shed 2. sheds 3. didn't shed 1. The other lamp shed a more agreeable light. 2. Most trees haven't shed their leaves yet.

Test 7: 1. said 2. has read* 3. rode* 4. have rung 5. rose 6. running 7. read* 8. ran 9. rode 10. don't shake 11. rose' 12. have seen 13. sell, sold 14. sent 15. sought 16. rose 17. has been shed* 18. shed

ÜBERSETZUNG: 1. Have you read the letter I wrote to you? 2. He rode as fast as he could. 3. He was run over by a van. 4. He said in his letter that he would come to see us in November. 5. I think I see your point. 6. I sold my flat to a rich man. 7. Last Thursday we finally sent our maid packing. 8. He was so frightened that he was shaking like a leaf. 9. She hasn't shed any of her bad habits.SHINE: 1. shone 2. shone* 3. shone* 1. The sun shines less in winter than in summer. 2. Yesterday the sun shone all day long. 3. Rise and shine! SHOOT: 1. shot* 2. shot 3. shot 1. He shot a glance at the book and put it away. 2. She shot quite a lot of photographs in Nepal. 3. We had to shoot this scene more than ten times. SHOW: 1. showed 2. haven't shown 3. show 1. How many times have I shown you how to boil eggs! 2. I don't understand why she hasn't shown up yet. 3. She never showed her feelings. SHRINK: 1. have shrunk* 2. shrank 1. As soon as you criticize him he shrinks into himself. 2. This shirt didn't use to be so tight; I'm sure it has shrunk. SHUT: 1. shut 2. haven't shut 3. shut 1. She shut the door because she felt cold. 2. He shut his eyes and imagined that he was lying on a palm beach. SING: 1. sang* 2. sang* 3. has sung* 1. Did your mother never sing you to sleep? 2. He sang quite a lot of beautiful songs in concert yesterday. 3. Did you sing Christmas carols this year? 4. We once had a parrot that didn't stop singing „Love me tender". SINK: 1. sank* 2. sank 3. have sunk 1. After his wife's death he sank into deep grief. 2. He sank onto the sofa and fell asleep. 3. I thought, this ship had sunk! SIT: 1. sit 2. sat 3. sit 1. She sat down in an armchair and began reading a book. 2. They were all sitting at the table, just waiting for me. 3. She sat on the floor and lit a candle. SLEEP: 1. slept 2. have slept 3. slept* 1. Have you just been sleeping? 2. Where did you sleep last night? 3. She said she had to sleep on it first. 4. He said he was still feeling tired although he had slept for ten hours. SMELL: 1. smelt/smelled 2. smelt/smelled 3. smelt/smelled 4. smelt/smelled 1. I smelt/smelled that he had cooked fish. 2. She was wearing a perfume that smelled/smelt of soap.

Test 8: 1. sitting 2. was shining 3. shut 4. shot, didn't shoot 5. sat 6. showed 7. have shrunk 8. shoots 9. hasn't shown 10. smelt/smelled* 11. sank 12. hasn't shrunk* 13. slept 14. sank

ÜBERSETZUNG: 1. You have to shine the lamp on the picture. 2. He was so desperate that he shot himself. 3. On Thursdays the shops won't shut before 8.30 p.m. 4. Billie Holiday sang in a lot of jazzclubs. 5. Have you ever sung a song by Gershwin on stage? 6. I can't understand why this painter has sunk into oblivion. 7. Don't sit up for me, I will be back late. 8. He was so fat that any chair he sat onto would break. 9. Her clothes always smell of the food she has been cooking.

SPEAK: 1. speaking 2. spoke 3. haven't spoken 1. My parents never spoke about their future. 2. She never used to speak about her boy-friend. 3. Have you spoken about your wage already? 4. Just dare to speak your mind! SPELL: 1. spell 2. have spelt 3. spelt/spelled 1. I asked her to spell her plan out for me. 2. Do you think I spelt this correctly? SPEND: 1. spent 2. spent 3. have spent 1. I'm afraid we have spent all the money we possessed 2. He spent all his money on a single day. 3. Where did you spend your last holiday? SPIN: 1. span/spun 2. spin 3. spin 1. Have you ever spun wool? 2. I have drunk too much beer and now my head is spinning. SPREAD: 1. spread 2. spread* 3. spread 1. He spread a blanket out onto the ground and lay down. 2. The bird spread its wings and flew away. 3. The cholera soon spread over the whole country. SPRING: 1. sprang 2. sprang 3. has sprung 1. Are you able to spring over this wall? 2. Suddenly the door sprang open. 3. The mistake sprang to his eyes immediately. STAND: 1. stand 2. stood 3. didn't stand 4. stood 5. stood 6. stood 7. stood

TEST 9: 1. sprang 2. did spend* 3. have spelt 4. spent* 5. stand 6. span/spun 7. spread 8. spoke 9. stood* 10. have spent

ÜBERSETZUNG: 1. Have you just been speaking about me? 2. Are you still not able to write my name correctly? I have already spelt it to you several times, haven't I? 3. How much money did you spend on your new bike? 4. Time span/spun away while he was telling his story. 5. The news about his engagement spread like wildfire through the village. 6. Why did you spring to your feet when I entered the room? 7. She stood up to her father.

STEAL: 1. stole* 2. have stolen 3. stole 4. stole* 1. I don't like my brother; he always steals the show from me. 2. I don't know where he got his new car from. He probably has stolen it. 3. Why did you steal this necklace? It is worthless! STICK: 1. stuck 2. stuck 3. stuck 1. Have you stuck the stamp on the letter already? 2. Unfortunately she didn't stick by me. 3. This has nothing to do with it. Please, stick to the point. STING: 1. stung* 2. stung* 3. sting 1. Her stinging remark hurt me very much. 2. I stung my finger with a needle. 3. Are you sure the scorpion stung you? STRIKE: 1. stroke 2. stroke 3. stroke 4. strike 1. I am glad he stroke the right note. 2. This picture struck my eye at once. 3. They were striking for higher wages. STRIVE: 1. strove 2. have always striven 1. In her youth she strove to become a ballet dancer. 2. Don't you think that she strove for happiness? 3. At that time I still strove for fame but now I know better. SWEAR: 1. sworn 2. swore 3. swore 1. I could have sworn that I had seen them together. 2. She always swore to tell the truth and then lied nevertheless. 3. He swore by all he holds dear so that I finally believed him. SWEAT: 1. sweat/sweated 2. sweat/sweated 3. have sweat/sweated 1. I sweat blood over this exam and failed it nevertheless. 2. I was surprised; I would never had thought that she would sweat it out. SWEEP: 1. swept 2. have swept 3. swept* 1. You could at least have swept the floor! 2. The flood swept away several houses. 3. You could have swept away his doubts so easily! SWIM: 1. swam* 2. swam* 3. swam* 1. She swam to the shore and broke down completely exhausted. 2. He swam faster than me and arrived first. 3. We swam to the little island and stayed there the whole day. SWING: 1. swing 2. swung 3. swung* 1. She swung round when I stepped into the room. 2. He rode through the pampas on a horse and swung his lasso. 3. He swung the lead yesterday. TAKE: 1. took 2. have taken 3. took 4. have taken 5. took* 6. took 7. took* 1. How many driving-lessons have you taken until now? 2. She just didn't take notice of him. 3. Just take your time! 4. Have you taken the letters to the post office already?

Test 10: 1. stole 2. stole 3. struck 4. stuck 5. struck 6. strove* 7. swore* 8. took 9. swept 10. sweat 11. sweat 12. struck 13. have taken 14. stuck 15. swept* 16. has swum 17. swam 18. swinging 19. swang 20. took

ÜBERSETZUNG: 1. The thieves have stolen everything we possessed. 2. His constant insults stung her. 3. He never strove towards perfection. 4. Suddenly, something swept across her mind.

TEACH: 1. taught* 2. have taught* 3. teach 1. Her parents haven't taught her how to behave well. 2. You haven't taught me the new game yet. 3. You could have taught your dog to open the door. TEAR: 1. tore 2. haven't torn 1. I could have torn my hair! 2. He tore the bill to pieces and left the restaurant. 3. You won't tear this cardboard so easily. TELL: 1. has told 2. told 3. told* 1. I know the situation looks desperate but you can never tell! 2. He told us he would go to America. 3. What has she just been telling you? THINK: 1. thought 2. have thought 3. thought 1. Who would have thought that! 2. He thought it would rain. 3. I would never have thought that we would meet again! 4. We thought you had left already. THROW: 1. thrown 2. did throw* 3. threw* 4. threw 1. Has this horse ever thrown you off? 2. As soon as he was in the street, he threw up. 3. His testimony throws new light on the murder. UNDERSTAND: 1. have understood* 2. understood 3. understood 1. I understand that you are a teacher. 2 You surely have understood me, haven't you. 3. Why doesn't she ever understand me? WEAR: 1. will wear* 2. wore* 3. worn 4. wore* 5. wore* 1. I think he wore a grey hat. 2. have you ever worn a beard? 3. Why don't you ever wear jeans? WEEP: 1. wept* 2. did weep* 3. weep 1. You shouldn't have wept out your eyes for her! 2. She wept herself to sleep every night. 3. Why did you weep when you saw her? 4. He wept over his fate a whole week. WIN: 1. won 2. won* 3. have won* 1. Who won the last match? 2. I placed all my money on the black horse but unfortunately it didn't win the race. 3. You could have won the prize easily. WRITE: 1. wrote* 2. wrote* 3. have written* 1. Why haven't you ever written to me in all these years? 2. Tennessee Williams wrote plays. 3. Who wrote the Bible? 4. He always wrote on red paper. 5. I don't recognize this handwriting; have you written this?

Abschlußtest:

1. haven't begun 2. bend 3. bit 4. has bitten 5. had broken 6. had burst 7. bursting 8. bought 9. has bought* 10. caught 11. have chosen 12. have clung 13. deals* 14. have dug 15. drew 16. drank 17. have felt 18. felt 19. fought 20. have fought 21. have found 22. haven't found 23. forgets 24. forgiven 25. frozen 26. got* 27. gave* 28. had gone 29. had 30. heard 31. hidden 32. knew* 33. leapt/leaped 34. lent 35. lay* 36. read 37. ride 38. ran 39. saw 40. haven't seen 41. have sought* 42. have sold 43. to send 44. to set 45. set 46. shook* 47. shook 48. shot 49. shot 50. shut 51. have sung* 52. sank 53. sat* 54. spoke 55. have spread 56. don't spread* 57. sprang 58. has taught 59. to teach 60. taught 61. tore* 62. have torn* 63. was torn 64. haven't told* 65. told 66. have thought 67. is thinking 68. had thought* 69. thrown 70. didn't understand 71. understood 72. wear 73. wept 74. won 75. won 76. won* 77. have won* 78. wrote 79. written 80. didn't write

Anhang: Die weiteren unregelmäßigen Verben

Die hier aufgelisteten Verben werden entweder nur noch selten in der englischen Sprache gebraucht, oder du kannst ihre Bildung aus anderen unregelmäßigen Verben ableiten.

abide	abode/abided	abode/abided	bleiben, wohnen
befall	befell	befallen	widerfahren
beget	begot	begotten	(er)zeugen
behold	beheld	beheld	erblicken
bereave	bereft/bereaved	bereft/bereaved	berauben
beseech	besought	besought	ersuchen
beset	beset	beset	besetzen; einschließen
bet	bet/betted	bet/betted	wetten
bid	bade/bid	bidden/bid	gebieten; lassen
blend	blended/blent	blended/blent	(sich)(ver)mischen
breed	bred	bred	züchten, hervorrufen
broadcast	broadcast/ed	broadcast/ed	durch Rundfunk senden
browbeat	browbeat	browbeaten	tyrannisieren
burn	burnt/burned	burnt/burned	brennen, verbrennen
chide	chid	chidden/chid	schelten
cleave	clove/cleft	cloven/cleft	spalten
dream	dreamt/dreamed	dreamt/dreamed	träumen
fling	flung	flung	werfen, schleudern
forbear	forbore	forborne	sich enthalten
forecast	forecast/ed	forecast/ed	vorhersagen
foresee	foresaw	foreseen	voraussehen, absehen
foretell	foretold	foretold	voraussagen
forsake	forsook	forsaken	aufgeben
gild	gilded/gilt	gilded/gilt	vergolden
gird	girded/girt	girded/girt	(um)gürten
grind	ground	ground	mahlen
heave	heaved/hove	heaved/hove	heben, hieven
hew	hewed	hewed/hewn	hauen, hacken
kneel	knelt	knelt	knien
knit	knitted/knit	knitted/knit	stricken
lade	laded	laden	laden
lean	leant/leaned	leant/leaned	(sich) lehnen
learn	learnt/leaned	learnt/learned	lernen, erfahren
melt	melted	melted/molten	schmelzen
mistake	mistook	mistaken	verwechseln
mow	mowed	mowed	mähen

overbear	overbore	overborne	überwältigen
overcome	overcame	overcome	überwältigen
partake	partook	partaken	teilnehmen
rend	rent	rent	zerreißen
rid	rid	rid	befreien
rive	rived	rived/riven	(sich) spalten
shear	sheared	sheared/shorn	scheren
shoe	shod	shod	beschuhen, beschlagen
slay	slew	slain	erschlagen
slide	slid	slid	gleiten (lassen)
sling	slung	slung	schleudern
slink	slunk	slunk	schleichen
smite	smote	smitten	treffen, schlagen
sow	sowed	sown	säen
speed	sped/speeded	sped/speeded	eilen, rasen
spill	spilt/spilled	spilt/spilled	vergießen
spit	spat	spat	spucken
split	split	split	spalten
spoil	spoilt/spoiled	spoilt/spoiled	verderben
stink	stank/stunk	stunk	stinken
strew	strewed	strewn	streuen
stride	strode	stridden	schreiten
swell	swelled	swollen	schwellen
thrive	throve	thriven	gedeihen
thrust	thrust	thrust	stoßen
tread	trod	trod(den)	treten
undergo	underwent	undergone	erleben, erdulden
upset	upset	upset	umwerfen, beunruhigen
weave	wove	woven	weben, flechten
wind	wound	wound	winden, wickeln
withdraw	withdrew	withdrawn	(sich) zurückziehen
withhold	withheld	withheld	zurückhalten
withstand	withstood	withstood	widerstehen
work	wrought	wrought	bewirken, (geistig) ausarbeiten
wring	wrung	wrung	(aus)wringen, ringen